A NEW GENERATION OF TROUT FLIES

FROM MIDGES TO MAMMALS
FOR ROCKY MOUNTAIN TROUT

A NEW GENERATION OF TROUT FLIES

FROM MIDGES TO MAMMALS FOR ROCKY MOUNTAIN TROUT

Scott Sanchez

Photography by Ted Fauceglia

First Edition

Library of Congress Cataloging-in-Publication Data
Sanchez, Scott.
A new generation of trout flies/Scott Sanchez.—1st ed.
p. cm.
ISBN 09746427-4-6 (hardcover)
Fly tying. 2. Fly fishing. I. Title.

Library of Congress Control Number: 2004117106

Book and cover design by Gregory Smith Design
Photographs of fly-tying steps and materials by Ted Fauceglia
Cover, pattern introduction, and fishing photos by the author

Published by Wild River Press, Post Office Box 13360, Mill Creek, Washington 98082 USA

Wild River Press Web site address: www.wildriverpress.com

Printed in Thailand

10 9 8 7 6 5 4 3 2 1

DEDICATION

For my son, Thibaud. May you keep enjoying the outdoors and the pleasures Nature brings. Let your curiosity travel this world.

Thibaud and Scott Sanchez take advantage of their neighborhood by fishing and making sand castles on a Snake River float. Jackson, Wyoming. July 2004

ACKNOWLEDGMENTS

Any project of this size requires the efforts of many. A number of people have made this book possible and enjoyable. Thanks to publisher Tom Pero and his new Wild River Press for asking me to write this book. Greg Thomas, thanks for inviting me to the Ennis on the Madison Fly-Fishing Festival and introducing me to Tom. A special thanks to Jack Dennis for introducing me to the fly-fishing public through his books and videos and for promoting me in his programs; an added thanks to Jack writing the Foreword during his extremely busy show and program season. Thanks to graphic designer Greg Smith for an outstanding book layout. Thanks to John Bailey for the opportunity to work on the Dan Bailey fly program and through doing so putting my patterns out to the world. Thanks to Ted Fauceglia for his wonderful step-by-step tying and materials photos. Thanks to Art Scheck for his valuable proof-reading. Finally, thanks each to fly-tying friends John Bailey, Dave Klausmeyer, Mike Lawson, Craig Mathews, and Shane Stalcup for taking time to look at my book and say a few kind words.

CONTENTS

FOREWORD

It is my great pleasure to introduce you to my friend and fellow fly tier Scott Sanchez. I have met many tiers during the 50 years I have spent at the vise, but very few are as creative and skilled as Scott.

And none has been as fun or as off the wall as "Chez," as his close friends call him. Cartoons have Gary Larson of *The Far Side* fame; fly fishing has Chez. Scott has a flare for the comical with such fanciful patterns as Santa Claus and the Christmas Tree, Bugs Bunny and the Ferrari sports car, and—my personal favorite—the Budweiser Frog complete with a six-inch tongue! One of the open secrets of the fly-fishing business is that most flies are made to catch fishers first and fish second. In his lighter moments of inspiration, Scott simply dispenses with all the pretense, much to the delight of all but the dullest of anglers.

While Scott loves to test the boundaries of fly tying for fun, it's the serious side of his imagination that *A New Generation of Trout Flies* is all about. From the lethal streamer the Double Bunny to the inventive Glass-House Caddis, Scott's trout patterns are lessons in creativity and practicality. Scott has crafted his patterns to be simple, durable imitations of insects and baitfish, with the use of materials many of us wouldn't have thought of using.

Good fishing and good friends: Scott Sanchez and Jack Dennis fishing the spring caddisfly hatch on the Yellowstone River near Livingston, Montana. May 2003

Several years ago, Scott made a video for me about understanding fly-tying materials. It's an excellent primer for any beginner trying to understand what he can use to make flies. Scott's many years of working at Dan Bailey's Fly Shop in Montana, where he ran the wholesale side of the materials business, has given him an unparalleled background in flies and materials from all corners of the Earth.

In recent years, Scott has written extensively for all the major fly-fishing magazines and has served as fly-tying editor for several. Altogether, the depth of Scott's experience and much-deserved recognition have vaulted him to the forefront of the national fly-tying scene.

As you will see in these pages, Scott Sanchez is a first-rate teacher. Whether you are a beginning, intermediate, or advanced tier, you will find that he makes things clear and easy to understand. In addition to learning new techniques, I suspect what you will really learn from this book is about Scott's passion for fly fishing, respect for nature, and his remarkable generosity. His willingness to share his knowledge with openness and refreshing humility is characteristic of the man—and the hallmark of this fine book.

For half a century now, I have been privileged to hold a front-row seat in watching the evolution of trout flies designed to fool wild Rocky

Mountain trout. *A New Generation of Trout Flies* is, I believe, an important milestone in this continuing journey.

With a fine mix of passion and humor and knowledge, Scott is about to guide you through his unique, whimsical world of trout flies. Get ready for enlightenment. Get ready also to learn about more than a few killer fly patterns. I assure you that when you reach the last page, you will emerge from your journey a more skilled fly tier and angler. Pay attention to the new Zen master.

Jack Dennis
Jackson Hole, Wyoming
January 2005

INTRODUCTION

My fly box is filled with ideas. I have gathered them from my own fishing experiences, from fly-tying experiments, from anglers I've guided, from other tiers, and from years of working in the fly-fishing business.

Many of the ideas were planned—answers to questions I was seeking. Some were gifts of fortune. Over the years, the evolution of my thinking about trout-fly design has led to the creation of an effective arsenal of working patterns that has consistently produced for me on my home waters and for other anglers around the world.

My flies catch fish. They reflect more than 20 years of living and fishing in the diverse greater Yellowstone region where the trout-rich states of Idaho, Montana, and Wyoming converge. This remarkable area is best known for large, free-flowing rivers, but this is only part of the picture. Smooth spring creeks with highly selective wild trout are scattered like jewels throughout the watersheds; freestone streams from small trickles to raging torrents are everywhere.

Sometimes the great fishing diversity of the Yellowstone country is found in a single watershed. On such a river the angler needs markedly different styles of flies to effectively fish the same hatch on the river's different water types. My Two-Tone Parachutes and Foam-Back Sparkle Duns, for example, cover the same mayflies, but each has advantages on certain types of water. The Yellowstone region also has a wide range of aquatic and terrestrial insects. Where else is it common to have size 4 salmonflies on the water next to size 18 pale morning duns? When fishing the South Fork of the Snake, you might be using a 7-weight, a sinking line, and a large streamer on one bank. As you move to the opposite side of the river, you switch to a 4-weight and a small dry. This leads to some different flies being created for the same piece of water. My Spandex Stone and Parachute Midge Emerger are very different flies, but both came from the Snake River.

Scott Sanchez at the oars of his trusty South Fork Skiff. Salt River, Wyoming. August 2004

With such demands for a wide range of flies, the chance for ideas to cross-mingle from different fly-tying disciplines is no accident. It's a given. Possibilities abound. The mind races. A tier who lives in an area where small imitative flies dominate the scene or in another place where large attractors get the big play isn't encouraged to experiment as much as I have been.

My flies are also influenced by the tying styles of this high country. Hair flies are standard throughout the West. This is perfectly logical. Natural hair—elk, deer, moose—is buoyant, durable, visible on finished flies, and easier to tie than many might think. My fondness for rabbit

Scott Sanchez, cold weather, a leech and a nice hybrid on Henry's Lake, Idaho. June 1996

comes from the bazillion Kiwi Muddlers I tied for Jack Dennis Sports in Jackson Hole. In recent years, foam has become a standard material in many everyday flies fished in the northern Rockies. These influences have found a home in many of my original fly patterns.

I'm often asked where my odd-material ideas come from. Originally, they came out of necessity. I grew up in Salt Lake City and learned to tie on my own. I ordered a rudimentary fly-tying kit from Herter's, and spent a lot of time at the library and reading fishing magazines. Since vast amounts fly-tying materials were not at my disposal and a 12-year-old's budget was limited, I learned to substitute. My mother's sewing and knitting boxes were common sources of supplies. I also gathered raw materials from neighbors who hunted or by keeping a constant lookout for road kills. If something looked like it would work for a fly, I tried it. I didn't have the option of tying every fly I saw by the book. Because of this, I think, experimenting was standard procedure. Although I didn't realize it during my formative years of tying, I became a more inquisitive—and more practical—designer of trout flies than if I had all the materials stocked by a typical modern fly shop at hand. The heart-shaped plastic beads I sometimes use for Double Bunny heads may not seem logical until you see them on a fly, but they look great and save time.

I have a reputation for being a synthetics junkie. While I do incorporate synthetics in many of my patterns, you will also find a great number of natural materials. Overall, I tie a lot of integrated flies. I believe a smart fly tier should use the material best suited for a particular part or function of a given fly. Flexibility in selecting materials can help in ease of tying,

Scott Sanchez entertaining and tying a Double Bunny at the Ennis on the Madison Fly-Fishing Festival. September 2004

flotation, density, or desired appearance. Dogmatic all-synthetic or all-natural tiers are missing out. My Foam-Wing Hopper is an attractive blend of the natural and the artificial.

Selling and writing about materials has contributed to my fly designs. This has given me the opportunity to see, touch, and experiment with more materials than the average tier. Also, when writing reviews of new materials, I sometimes need to dream up less-traditional uses of some materials to show their worth to a wide range of tiers. That can inspire innovative approaches.

I'm fortunate to have worked in the fly-fishing industry since I was 14. My experience includes just about everything: designing flies, teaching classes, guiding, waiting on customers in retail fly shops, filling mail orders, servicing wholesale sales, traveling as a sales representative, working as a tackle consultant, and cranking out fly orders. I know my flies work well beyond the Rocky Mountains, and wish I had as many frequent-flier miles as my fly patterns.

You can learn a lot from other anglers, and contact with them greatly expands your knowledge of what works in flies. Sometimes the obvious is hard to see from the inside. Feedback from others helps you to adapt and improve your flies. In some cases, tying clients are the catalyst for certain flies. The idea for my Convertible came from numerous requests for a super-versatile pattern that would hold up in the Jackson Hole One-Fly competition; it has become one of my best attractor patterns.

Commercial tying changes your perceptions of fly tying. One thing you learn pretty quickly is that time is indeed money. It's the biggest expense in making large numbers of trout flies. This also means that if you want to spend more time fishing, tying flies should be time-efficient. I don't want complicated or time-consuming patterns, because then I have to produce them. A commercial tier develops many speedy shortcuts. If these techniques also improve your flies, all the better. My Ultra Zug came from a need for a quick, disposable nymph. Now the clump-dubbing method I developed is also used in some of my other flies.

Overall, you'll see that my flies are representative creations rather than exact imitations. I believe strongly that an artificial fly shouldn't be more complicated than the natural it pretends to duplicate. A quality trout fly should feature the most important triggers for an effective fly, while being reasonably straightforward in design. Key triggers are color, size, profile, and movement. Ask a four-year-old what he sees in an

Scott Sanchez enjoying a float on his home water of the Snake River. September 2004

insect and you will probably get the most important characteristic—and that's exactly what you should highlight. The yellow horizontal stripe on the Light Stone Biot Bug is a feature that feeding trout key on during *Isoperla* stonefly hatches, and the olive glass bead on the Glass-House Caddis is an exaggeration of the green caddisfly larva inside its case.

Saltwater and warmwater fishing has expanded my perspective on fly design. There is a lot to be learned by pulling from different directions. Fishing for different species helps gives you different insights and broadens your knowledge of fishing techniques. Many of these can be adapted back into the trout world. My Double Bunny may not have been created if it wasn't for a flats trip to Belize. Fishing for pike and bass with a fly has given me great insights into predator-prey relationships.

Evolution may be the most important part of revolution. It is hard to come up with a unique fly pattern. We have been imitating the same insects with roughly the same materials for centuries, but modifying flies can help us to create more effective imitations. And sometimes showing the fish something a little different will increase takes. My Everything Emerger evolved from Craig Mathews's wonderful X Caddis, as I learned that most cripples have a similar profile regardless of species.

Fly fishing and tying seem so intertwined. I couldn't imagine fly fishing without tying flies. It is immensely satisfying to be able to create a fly to fill a specific fishing need, to experiment and explore fresh directions in combining familiar and unfamiliar materials in new ways.

May it never end.

SCOTT SANCHEZ
JACKSON HOLE, WYOMING
January 2005

CHAPTER 1

MATERIALS AND HOOKS

MATERIALS MAKE THE FLY. Just as in any other manufacturing, whether by hand or machine, the finished product will be only as good as the raw materials. In addition, good materials make tying easy while bad materials make it frustrating. Just as important as good materials are *correct* materials for the job. I'll give you a quick overview of some the materials that will be used in the fly patterns you'll be learning how to tie in this book.

Hooks

Hooks are the core of any fly. Fortunately, it has never been easier to find premium product. Unfortunately, the vast array of good options can leave a tier very confused. I think I own a good chunk of the models on the market, but I actually use only a few of them. A good approach for most tiers is to pick a brand of hooks and then narrow down the range of models to what you need, rather than having a jumble of hooks that duplicate each other. I've worked with Dai-Riki for years—this is my brand preference. But Daiichi, Mustad, and Tiemco are also good, commonly available hooks.

My hook base includes a standard dry-fly hook (Dai-Riki 320); a light-wire emerger hook (Dai-Riki 125); a standard-shank, heavy-wire nymph hook (Dai-Riki 075); a slightly longer, heavy-wire nymph hook for bead heads (Dai-Riki 060); a light-wire, long-shank, natural bend hook (Dai-Riki 270); a standard-wire, long-shank, natural-bend hook (Dai-Riki 280); and a long-shank streamer hook (Dai-Riki 700). I certainly use other hooks for specific purposes, but most trout flies can be tied with these.

Thread

Thread is the critical link between your hook and the materials. Today's fly tier is blessed with a large number of good products, and confused by the mass at the same time. The "0" system of measurement (6/0, 8/0, and so on) is a good reference only within one brand, and the universal textile-industry Denier measurement is listed on only some threads.

A few years ago I was commissioned to write an article about threads for the Japanese magazine *Tightloop*. Through experience, research, inside information, and measurement, I was able to get a good thread rating. It isn't exact, because thread isn't, but it is close enough to be functional. Within the following categories, the threads are close enough in size and strength to perform the task.

I find Gudebrod 8/0 and 10/0 thread invaluable for small flies. They allow the tier to make secure, small flies without bulk. The waxed versions of UNI 6/0 and 8/0 are very tough and are not easily cut by rough bead heads. The flat, floss-like nylon threads from Danville and Wapsi come in vibrant colors and can be used in place of floss. I didn't include Kevlar or GSP threads in the following list. They are incredible strong, but I don't like how they tie.

BEST FOR VERY SMALL FLIES AND SPARSE BODIES

Gudebrod 10/0
Gudebrod 8/0

BEST FOR SIZES 10 TO 22 TROUT FLIES AND FOR AVOIDING BULK ON LARGER FLIES

Benecchi 12/0
Griffiths 14/0
Wapsi Ultra 70
UNI 8/0
Danville Flymaster 6/0

BEST FOR MEDIUM-SIZE TROUT FLIES, FINE HAIR WORK, AND FLIES WITH HEAVY OR COARSE MATERIALS

Griffiths 8/0
Benecchi 10/0
Danville 3/0 Monocord
Benecchi 8/0
Wapsi Ultra 140
Gudebrod 3/0
Uni 6/0

HIGH-STRENGTH THREADS FOR BIG FLIES AND HAIR BUGS

Danville Size A Monocord
Gudebrod G
Danville Flat Waxed Nylon
Danville Flymaster+
Wapsi Ultra 210
Wapsi Ultra 280

Hair

I live in hair-fly country, and hair is an integral part of many of my fly patterns. The correct hair and quality hair will improve the appearance of your fly; it will make a pattern easier to tie and will make it fish better. Regardless of the kind of hair you're tying with, the following characteristics are important in selecting it.

1. Look for straight hair. Hair with curvature is more difficult to even up for making neat wings and tails. The curvature we are talking about isn't the crinkle in the hair, such as that in calf tail, but the overall drape of the hair.

2. You don't want broken natural tips on the hair. If the tips are broken, you will never be able to tie a neat-looking fly.

3. Look for hair that is long enough to easily tie with. A little extra length at the base of the hair will make it easier to secure.

After these attributes, matching the hair to the purpose is important. Today's dyeing techniques allow you to accurately imitate most food forms.

Natural hair off the hide doesn't have even tips. On the animal, the staggered filaments acts like shingles on the roof of a house. This helps shed water and helps camouflage the creature. When we tie a fly, we want to even up the tips of the hair. This is for us, not the fish. Humans like neat-looking flies. This is accomplished by dropping the hair into a hair evener or "stacker," as it's commonly called. Gravity and momentum align the tips.

Natural hair has underfur, which insulates the animal, but also makes hair hard to even. Clean this out with your fingers or a comb. When you are cleaning out this underfur, you may feel like you are wasting material, but you are saving yourself a headache.

Hair comes in many textures, which can create different looks and functions on a fly. The more hollow the hair, the easier it is to spin or flare. Less-hollow hair is more durable and supports the fly better. Hollow hair is like a plastic straw; solid hair is like a pencil. If you push down on the straw, the ends will pop up—if you push down on the pencil, nothing happens. Natural hair varies from animal to animal. There is sometimes an overlap in the use of hair in constructing trout flies. The following hairs are those I use most often.

CALF TAIL: Calf-tail fibers are from 3/4 of an inch to 2 inches long and crinkled. I use calf tail for wings on Trudes and Convertibles. The crinkle in it makes a wing look full with less material, and gives it floatation. One trick for cleaning up calf tails is to brush them with a wire dog brush. This straightens and cleans up the fibers.

ELK MANE: This is the long hair from the neck of a bull elk. It is fairly fine and a good material for dry-fly tails. It can also be wrapped as a body.

MOOSE BODY: This hair is used as tails on many hairwing dry flies. It is a medium-thickness hair and fairly stiff. It can also be used as antennae.

BULL ELK: This is sold as light elk. It is a medium-fine to medium-thickness hair. It is used on numerous dry flies. It is used as a wing in tying the Elk Hair Caddis. It also makes a good parachute wing. I prefer it over deer for small Comparaduns. Elk is more hollow at the tips and easier to tie in without bulk. Bull elk is good for extended bodies, too. It is the most durable of the "hollow" hairs. It is available in a natural sand color with gray butts and in many dyed-over-colors.

COW ELK: This is sold as dark elk. It is medium to medium-coarse in diameter. It has sand-color tips with a gray color through the rest of the fiber. It is used as dry-fly wings. It is a more durable substitute for deer on bullet-head dries. It is available in natural gray, bleached, or dyed over bleached.

DEER: Body hair from deer living in northern climates is the most popular hair for spinning. You can get almost any deer-body hair to flare at its base, but, as you move up the hair, it will get finer and less hollow. This happens as the hair changes in color from the gray of the butts to the tan or brown of the tips. You won't be able to flare the hair in this fine section. When selecting hair for flies with a collar (Muddlers and their like), make sure the hollow section of the hair lets you tie the length of collar you desire. With the wrong hair, you might have to tie a size 6 collar on a size 10 fly. Both whitetail and mule deer can be used for flaring, but I give a slight edge to whitetail. Look for hair with the least amount of underfur.

SNOWSHOE RABBIT FOOT: The hair from this critter makes great almost unsinkable dry flies. It is limited in length and can't be evened, but it makes buggy-looking wings that float even after catching a few fish.

Dubbing

Dubbing, although an ancient method of making a fly body, is still an important technique to today's tier. One advantage of dubbing is that there is no tie-in or tie-off point. This means no bulk in those areas. Bodies can be tapered to form natural-looking insect bodies and can be put onto a hook sparser than with other materials. This is especially important on small patterns.

Dubbing comes in different textures. A fine denier is used on small flies or when a smooth body is called for. Coarser dubbings are used to give a shaggy, buggy effect on nymphs and some dry flies. The trick to dubbing is to put very small amounts of it on the thread and then add more onto the previous layer. If you put too much on the thread, the fibers will have difficulty adhering. Also, when putting the dubbing on, pinch it with pressure as you roll it on. You won't break the thread by rolling it.

FINE DUBBINGS: Some common synthetics are Wapsi Superfine, Scintilla Micro-Fibre, and Fine & Dry. Wapsi Beaver Dubbing or Stalcup's Micro Fine Dry Fly Dub are good options if you prefer a fine natural dubbing. These dubbing make it possible to tie minute flies.

COARSER DUBBINGS: I use these medium-sized synthetic dubbings for dry and wet flies on which I want a rougher body texture. Some common brands are Scintilla, Sparkle Dub, Synthetic Living Fibre (SLF), and a variety of Antron blends. I like these for my Ultra Zug series and Clump Dubbing leeches. Dubbings listed as leech dubbing or leech blends are also good for clump dubbing. I use Scintilla Peacockle dubbing in place of peacock herl almost exclusively. It looks the same on a finished fly and it is much tougher.

FLASH DUBBING: The fine Mylar dubbings have become very popular for nymphs and baitfish patterns. They are nice when a flashy, tapered body is desired. They can also be used as shucks and wings. Some of the common varieties are Flashabou Dubbing, Lite Brite, and Angel Hair. The new finer Mylars such as Ice Dub and Polar Dub can be used on very small flies.

In general, finer dubbing adheres to thread more easily, while heavier, coarser material will give your fly a buggy look.

Rubber

Rubber legs have become a mainstay tying material. They give motion and a realistic profile to some patterns. I use a variety of rubbers.

Round rubber is the standard rubber leg material. In appearance it looks like a number of round filaments fused together at the edges. This structure makes it very simple to divide individual legs. It is generally sold in three sizes in white, black, and natural (latex cream). The medium size comes in a multitude of colors. The colors in round rubber are vibrant.

When I need rubber legs with muted colors, I use the traditional square rubber legs, also called live rubber or living rubber. These are long sheets of perforated rubber, which can be divided into multiple strands. I like to use them when I want to add color without overdoing it, and I find some of the colors invaluable. They are a little harder to separate into strands than round rubber. This can be good and bad. This is good if you are knotting multiple strands into legs, such as on a hopper, since they will hold together better. The bad part is they require more effort and time to split.

Angler's Choice Bodeez 'N' Legz or Hedron Perfect Rubber look similar to silicone rubber legs, but are stronger and naturally buoyant.

Start by Choosing the Correct Hook for the Shape of Your Fly

Standard Dry-Fly Hook

Double-Vision PMD

The Dai-Riki model 320 shown here features a uniform gap throughout its range of sizes. A perfect choice for conventional and parachute dry flies.

Eye: Down
Wire: Standard
Length: 1X Long
Bend: Round
Finish: Bronze
Sizes: 8 to 24

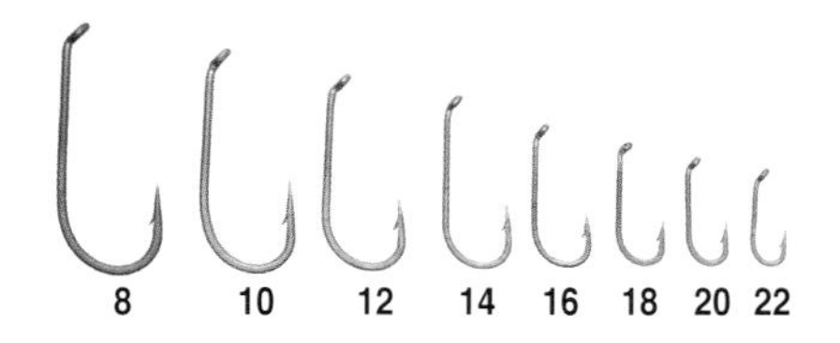

Natural-Bend 3XL Hook

Foam-Wing Hopper

The Dai-Riki model 270 with its special bend gives the fly a natural look. Use on patterns such as Stimulators, hoppers, caddisflies, and nymphs.

Eye: Straight
Wire: Standard
Length: 3X Long
Bend: Special
Finish: Bronze
Sizes: 4 to 24

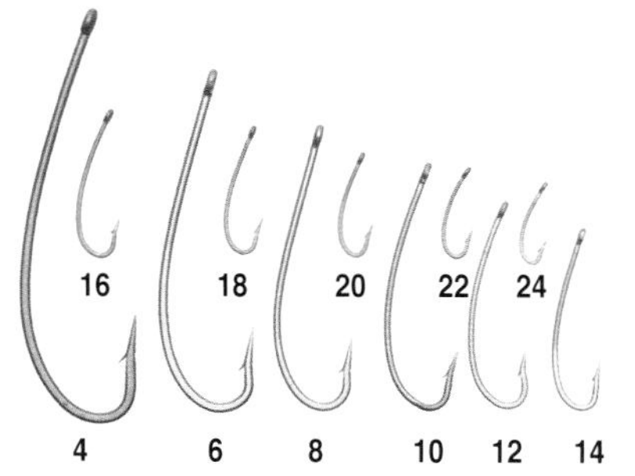

Emerger Hook

Midge X

The Dai-Riki model 125 features a 2X short shank, straight eye, and reversed bend. It is ideally suited for parachute emergers, nymphs, and caddisfly patterns.

Eye: Straight
Wire: Standard
Length: 2X Short
Bend: Reversed
Finish: Bronze
Sizes: 12 to 24

12 14 16 18 20 22 24

Natural-Bend 2XL Hook

Spandex Stone

The Dai-Riki model 280 features a 2X long, slightly curved shank, making it ideal for stoneflies, hoppers, and larger bead-head nymphs.

Eye: Down
Wire: Standard
Length: 2X Long
Bend: Round
Finish: Bronze
Sizes: 6 to 16

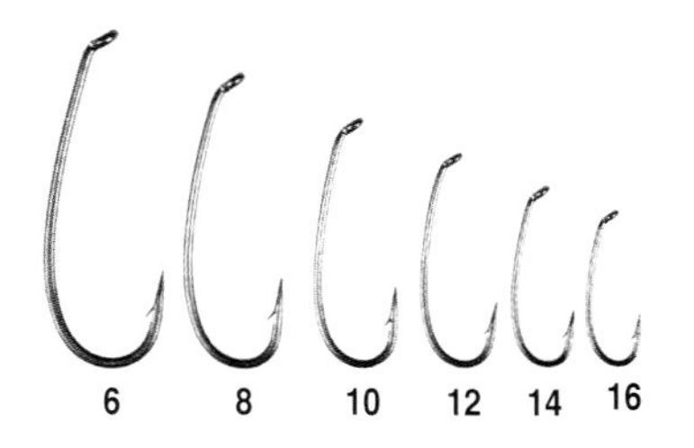

Streamer Hook

Double Bunny

The Dai-Riki model 700 is used when you require a longer shank to tie streamers, Woolly Buggers, nymphs, and other long-bodied patterns.

Eye: Down
Wire: 1X Strong
Length: 4X Long
Bend: Round
Finish: Bronze
Sizes: 1 to 16

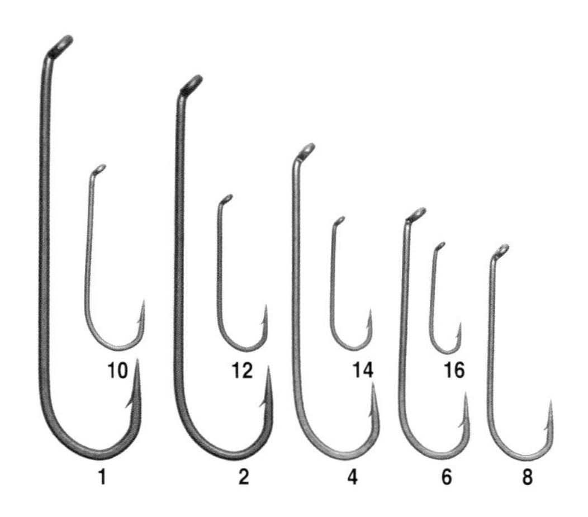

Nymph 1XL Hook

Glass-House Caddis

The Dai-Riki model 060 is a 1X long nymph hook that is perfect for most mayfly nymph bodies and emerger patterns.

Eye: Down
Wire: 1X Strong
Length: 1X Long
Bend: Sproat
Finish: Bronze
Sizes 6 to 22

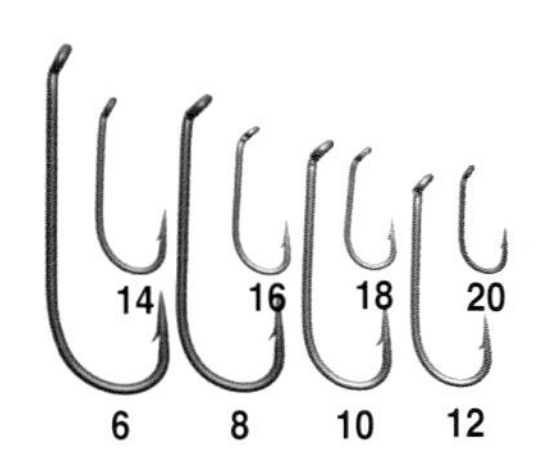

Scud/Pupa Hook

Teal Baetis Nymph

With its curved shank and slightly offset bend, the Dai-Riki model 135 is the perfect choice for scuds, caddis pupae and larvae.

Eye: Down
Wire: 1X Strong
Length: 1X Short
Bend: Reversed
Finish: Bronze
Sizes: 6 to 22

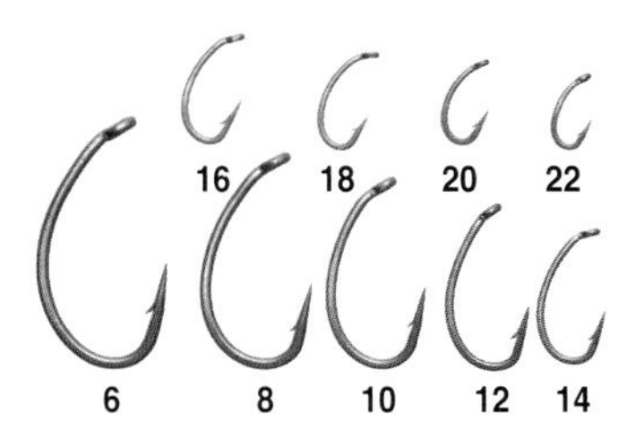

Nymph 1XS Hook

Ultra Zug

The Dai-Riki model 075 provides maximum strength for big fish. The heavy wire also aids in getting a fly down fast.

Eye: Down
Wire: 2X Strong
Length: 1X Short
Bend: Sproat
Finish: Bronze
Sizes: 8 to 20

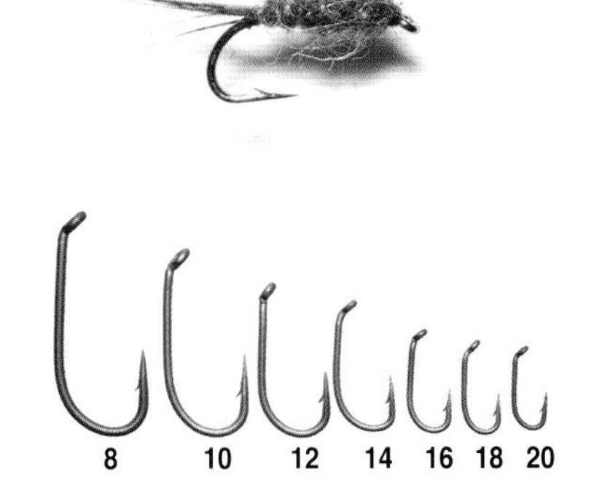

All hooks shown are actual size

Leading Manufacturers' Comparable Hook Designs

Hook Style	Dai-Riki	Mustad	Tiemco	Daiichi
Standard Dry Fly	320	94840	100	1180
Emerger	125	N/A	2488	1130
Natural-Bend 3XL	270	AC80050BR	200R	1270
Natural-Bend 2XL	280	94831	2302	1280
Streamer 4XL	700	79580	9395	2220
Scud/Pupa	135	AC80200BR	2457	1150
Nymph 1XL	060	3906B	3761	1560
Nymph 1XS	075	N/A	3796	1530

They are round polyurethane filaments with a textured finish. If you want buggy, mottled colors or translucent legs, these are nice. They make great extended bodies on midges or small caddisflies.

Spandex is a strong rubberized filament; it's the most flexible for the diameter. It looks like floss. It's sold under names such as Flexi Floss, Super Floss, and Spanflex. Spandex comes in many dyed colors and it can be easily dyed or colored with permanent markers. It can be purchased in different diameters, or the filaments can be split with a bodkin. Because of its limpness, it is excellent for mobile wet flies. However, this soft texture won't support large dry flies on the surface. And when you twitch a fly, Spandex won't rebound back to its shape like other rubbers. Its best uses are on subsurface flies that are meant to be dead-drifted or retrieved slowly, or on small dries. It will absorb water or floatant. It has other uses beyond legs. It can be used as durable floss that won't change color when wet and as wing cases or shellbacks.

Rabbit

I really like the action rabbit fur gives to flies. The fish seem to agree. A common misconception about selecting rabbit for rabbit-strip flies is to look for the longest hair. Hair that is around an inch long will give as much action as longer hair, but sinks quicker and it is easier to cast—two valuable characteristics of a streamer.

Rabbit is sold in various configurations. There are whole hides (they make rabbits that way); 1/8-inch Zonker or rabbit strips; 1/4- to 3/8-inch Magnum, Kiwi, or Big Boy strips; and cross cut strips. The 1/8-inch strips are popular for Zonkers or strip leeches, while the wider strips are better for Double Bunnies, tails, saltwater patterns, and bass flies. These products are cut with the grain of the hair. Cross-cut strips are 1/8 of an inch wide but are cut across the hide. They are wrapped as a rabbit hackle. You can cut your own strips from a hide, but this requires caution so that you don't cut human strips. I use a disposable box-cutter knife.

Foam

I use closed-cell foam as part of many dry flies. It adds buoyancy to dry-fly patterns. Flat foam comes in different thicknesses; the 2 mm craft-style foam is the most common. This product is sold in a wide range of colors and can be laminated for two-tone bodies and wings. Use a spray contact adhesive, such as 3M Super 77. The new .5 mm and 1 mm foams, such as Wapsi Razor Foam, expanded the range of foam in fly tying. It is now practical to use foam on delicate spring-creek flies. Wrightway Sports has recently started producing pre-made Foam-Wing Caddis wings.

Synthetic Yarns

Antron, Z-Lon, Para Post, Darlon, and Hi-Vis Floater are similar fibers with similar purposes. The original Antron was popularized by the late Gary LaFontaine in his effective patterns. I use these products interchangeably as parachute posts, wings, and trailing shucks. They also make an excellent floss substitute that won't change color when it gets wet. For shucks and posts, I like the coarser products with a little crinkle in them. The fibers on these don't mat as easily, and they also give a better profile.

Flash

I use Mylar flash on both wet and dry flies. It adds motion and a minnowlike appearance to streamers, but it also is useful for wings and dry-fly posts. The sheen looks like some insect wings and adds some visibility for the angler. Flash is sold in pearlescent, metallic, and holographic shades and comes in two common forms: flat and twisted. Flashabou is the most common flat product and it comes in a wide range of colors. Hareline's Krystal Flash is the prominent twisted Mylar, and a finer Midge Flash is sold by Wapsi Fly. The twisted flashes give off more of a scaled appearance, while the flat is more mobile. The twisted flash is slighter stiffer; it's bulkier in appearance and it makes better dry-fly wings. Also, the twisted flashes are tougher when used as a rib.

Adhesives

I'm a glue junkie. The discreet use of adhesives will make your flies more durable and better looking.

For head cement, my favorite is nail polish. It dries quickly and gives the heads on flies a nice glossy finish. I save the thickened bottles for glossy heads on streamers. Dave's Flexament is a good head-cement product. To prevent your flies from twisting, cement the hook shank before starting your thread. This is very important on hair and foam flies. I'm not a fan of water-based head cements. They take too long to dry and I find that they aren't as secure. Also, just because they say water-based doesn't mean they are environmentally benign.

Cyanoacrylate glues or "super glues" are terrific for fusing flies together. Use a disposable bodkin or toothpick to apply them sparingly. I sometimes coat Double Bunny heads with a five-minute epoxy. If you have a rotisserie or fly turner it isn't difficult; if you don't, I wouldn't bother. The glue I use for laminating Double Bunny rabbit hides is called Val-A Tearmender. This is a pure rubber-tree latex and it is nicer to work with than solvent-based contact cements. It can be bought at hardware or canvas-repair shops, and it is distributed to fly shops by Hareline and Freestone Flies. Goop, Shoe Goo, and Zap A Gap A Doo II are clear, pliable adhesives and the best things I've found for gluing eyes on streamers. I use double-stick carpet tape to secure the foam on my Foam-Wing Hopper. It prevents cutting the foam and flaring it.

MAYFLIES

THE GREATER YELLOWSTONE REGION HAS GOOD POPULATIONS and varieties of mayflies. They range from size 22 Tricos to size 10 brown drakes and everything in between. The area also has a wide range of water types and sizes. Small freestone streams, spring creeks, lakes, and large rivers all have decent populations of mayflies. Waters such as the Henry's Fork have about any kind of mayfly you could imagine; multiple hatches at the same time are common. This river has been responsible for more match-the-hatch patterns than any other water I know.

One of the most interesting aspects of western angling is fishing small mayflies on large rivers. Large rivers such as the South Fork of the Snake, Madison, Missouri, and Yellowstone—in and out of the national park—have great hatches of small mayflies.

Double-vision Pale Morning Dun

One might associate these bigger rivers only with attractors and big flies. That's a mistake, and at times match-the-hatch fishing with mayflies is critical to success. For example, a size 20 dry and a 6X tippet may seem out of place on a river with a flow of 3,000 cubic feet per second, but sizable Missouri River rainbows don't think so. Much of this fishing happens in riffles, inside corners, and tailouts, where the rising fish can be more selective than one would expect. Conditions can vary from smooth tailouts to choppy water, but every type of water requires accurate imitations.

It is important to dissect these rivers into smaller pieces to fish them effectively. Large fish can sometimes be found in very skinny water, and many anglers spook bankside fish while wading. Side channels offer fine fishing and can make a big river feel like a small creek. On some rivers, such as the South Fork, some of the best mayfly fishing can be found in riffles in the middle of the river. However, to fish many of these places requires a boat.

One factor that comes into play on many Montana rivers is their direction of flow: north. The sun moves from east to west, which can make all but midday visibility tough. There is a terminal white-silver glare on the water. High-visibility patterns can lead to better presentations and make the angler confident in his fly. The Two-Tone Parachutes were design to deal with this situation while providing a realistic profile for the trout.

The most important western mayflies, because of their ubiquitous range and longevity of emergence, are *Ephemerella infrequens* and *inermis*, commonly called pale morning duns (PMD), and a variety of *Baetis* species, or blue-winged olives (BWO).

Their seasons overlap, with BWOs being primarily spring and fall hatches and PMDs covering the summer months. Both hatches are long-lived, so fish get a chance to key into them as well as become selective to them. In general, PMDs get smaller as the season progresses, with size16 at the beginning and size 22 at the end.

Other common river mayflies are flav (*Drunella flavilinea*), March brown (*Rhithrogena morrisoni*), gray drake (*Siphlonurus occidentalis*), Trico (*Tricorythodes*), yellow quill, red quill, and pink Albert (Heptageniidae), mahogany dun (*Paraleptophlebia*), and *Callibaetis*. Though less common, green drakes (*Drunella grandis*) and brown drakes (*Ephemera simulans*) can be locally significant.

With the variety of water types found here, I sometimes use different styles of dry flies to imitate the same insect. Wulffs and heavily hackled parachutes are perfect for the pocket water of high-mountain streams or swift runs on large rivers; their buoyancy and visibility are well suited to the fast water. Low-floating, sparse patterns are better for critical fish in the smooth waters of a spring creek or tailwater.

We do a lot of float fishing in my area, and we often use different patterns when floating than we use when we are wading. While floating, I use larger, more buoyant and visible flies. The fish get one look at the fly and are generally less critical of the imitation. When we stop and work a pod of fish, flies that are correctly sized and more exact representations are a better choice. When one casts repeatedly to fish, they become less tolerant of less-imitative flies. During July, mayflies are common on most waters and mayfly patterns can be good searching flies.

It is important to dissect these rivers into smaller pieces to fish them effectively. Large fish can sometimes be found in very skinny water.

With mayflies hatching from March through October, anglers fishing the West have a good a chance of fishing a hatch and should have a range of mayfly imitations in their vests.

Double-Vision Flies

Good, accurate drifts are an important factor in match-the-hatch fishing. While the color, size and shape of the fly help fool the fish, a natural presentation is an essential part of the equation—it may be

DOUBLE-VISION PALE MORNING DUN

HOOK:	Dai-Riki 320 standard dry fly, sizes 14 to 20.
THREAD:	Light olive 8/0 or 10/0.
WING:	Black and yellow Antron.
HACKLE:	Dyed PMD or light dun.
TAILS:	Tan Microfibbetts.
BODY:	Pale yellow dubbing.

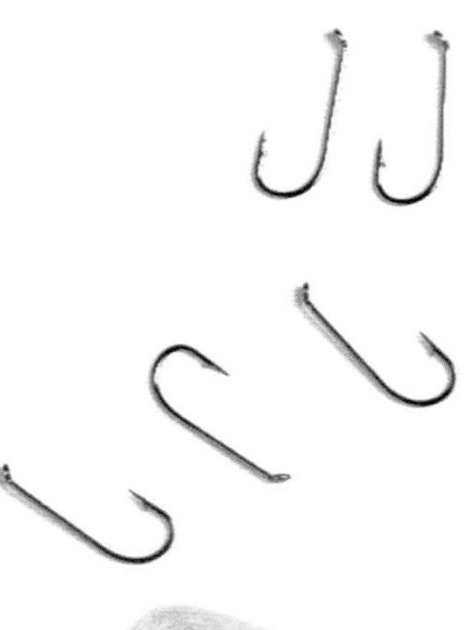

Different wing colors work in different conditions, and those that contrast against the background will be the easiest to see.

the most important trigger. Without a good drift, the best-looking fly in the world won't produce. Flies that are easy to follow let you know if your drift is good or bad, and whether the fly is in the correct spot. They also help prevent striking when a trout rises to a real insect and consequently putting down an actively rising fish. As I get older, I no longer make fun of people who have difficulty seeing flies: I've become one of them.

Different wing colors work in different conditions, and those that contrast against the background will be the easiest to see. The traditional white wing is good when viewed against a dark bottom or in shaded areas. However, against silvery surface glare it gets lost. Black wings provide good profile and contrast under these conditions, but are hard to see against a dark bottom or undercut bank. Orange, pink, yellow, and chartreuse are other visible alternatives; they stand out in many conditions and make your fly distinguishable from naturals during heavy hatches. Hot pink is one of my favorites.

The fisherman's angle of view sometimes changes the background color and, consequently, the best wing choice. For example, an angler standing in a drift boat may be looking down at the fly against the background of the river bottom, while, in the same water, a deep-wading angler might be watching his fly against the sheen of the water surface or the backdrop of the far bank. Wings that are visible in many conditions can help angling success.

My friend Johnny Boyd told me about some Montana tiers using the ends of Rainy's Hi-Viz Ant Bodies for a multi-colored post. With the bright tip and black base, they can use the same fly to fish different light conditions. This sounded good, but I could go through an outrageous number of pricey bodies. And while I like short foam posts for emergers and spinners, they don't look quite right on dun-length wings. Also, the optimum flat, light wing would have a black tip and a bright base as opposed to the reversed pattern on the ant-body parachutes. The black is set on top to provide a silhouette for both the trout and the angler to see.

I let his idea sit for a while, but as spring *Baetis* time approached, the idea came back to me. Blue-winged olives always seem to hatch in the worst light conditions.

I tried permanent marker on synthetic fibers, but many floatants will fade or remove the marker. I kept thinking it would be great to have a material with perfect black tips and a bright base. While tying an order of Tarantulas with golden pheasant tippet tails, the idea literally fell into my lap. Nature had already created a winging material with pronounced black tips and a bright base!

I first tried golden pheasant, but quickly found that dyed Amherst pheasant tippets were better, since they are softer and more opaque, and the dyed-over-white fluorescent colors are brighter. The best tippets I've found for small flies are the white ring feathers on the neck of a ringneck pheasant. Some of them have black tips. Dyed versions are sold as exotic-feather substitutes for Atlantic salmon flies. A look around the tying bench may find other suitable feathers.

My flies are always evolving—the Two-Tone Parachute is no exception. When Dan Bailey's Fly Shop decided to produce the fly commercially, the availability of mass quantities of nicely dyed tippets was an issue. I needed to figure out a viable bulk option. I went back to the synthetics and tied a parachute with a tiered Antron post. This gave the same effect as the multicolored feather, but wing colors and supply were unlimited. This also allows the option of having the indicator at the base or the top of the wing. I still fish some of the feather flies, but I find synthetic flies more buoyant. Also, when viewing the fly from the front, the wider wing is easier to see. Antron and poly are the most common synthetic post materials, but other materials can be used. The Double-Vision Parachutes have become some of Dan Bailey's most popular patterns, so others must be benefiting from their enhanced performance. Give these flies a try. They might double your odds.

Rotating hackle pliers such as those made by Griffin or Tiemco make it easier for most tiers to wrap parachute hackle.

Cement the hook shank, start your thread, and make a thread base on the hook. Behind the eye of the hook at a distance equal to one-quarter the length of the shank, tie in a strand of black Antron; secure it in the center of the material.

Lift up the ends and securely post them to make a wing. Make many thread wraps to create a solid base on which to wrap the hackle.

Pull the yellow Antron up from under the shank of the hook and post to secure it to the underwing. Make it longer than the center color—this will make it easier to trim later on.

Trim the outer wing to length by pulling each side and trimming it away from the center color. Doing each side individually is much easier than trying to trim it all at once. It should be three-quarters of a shank length, and shorter than the center color.

Trim the center, black wing so it is a shank-length long and slightly longer than the yellow.

Tie the hackle in behind the wing. It will extend past the eye of the hook. Leave it to wrap later. The fibers of your hackle should be equal to one and a half times the hook gap.

Make a dubbing loop with the thread and secure it at the bend of the hook. One thread strand should be on each side of the hook.

Tie in Microfibbett tails over the dubbing loop. Use four to six fibers; they should be a shank-length long after affixing them to the hook.

Push down with a fingernail to split the tails, and pull the dubbing loop up through the tails to separate them. Secure the dubbing loop with tying thread. Leave the excess dubbing loop for the rib.

Dub a slender abdomen up to the post.

Twist the dubbing-loop thread and use it to rib the body.

Figure-eight-wrap dubbing around the wing to make a thorax. Wrap dubbing slightly up the wing to make a base for the hackle.

Wrap the hackle. Make one counterclockwise wrap up the post and make the rest of the wraps under the first one.

To tie off the hackle, drop your hackle pliers over your tying thread, and then point the tip of your bobbin toward the post. Reel in your bobbin. Lightly jiggle your bobbin. This allows the thread to work up through the hackle fibers to the hackle stem without catching the fibers.

Secure the hackle to the hook shank. Keep your bobbin tip close to the shank. Pull with your bobbin when the thread is under the hook shank, but as you come over the shank, point with your bobbin so that the thread goes under the hackle.

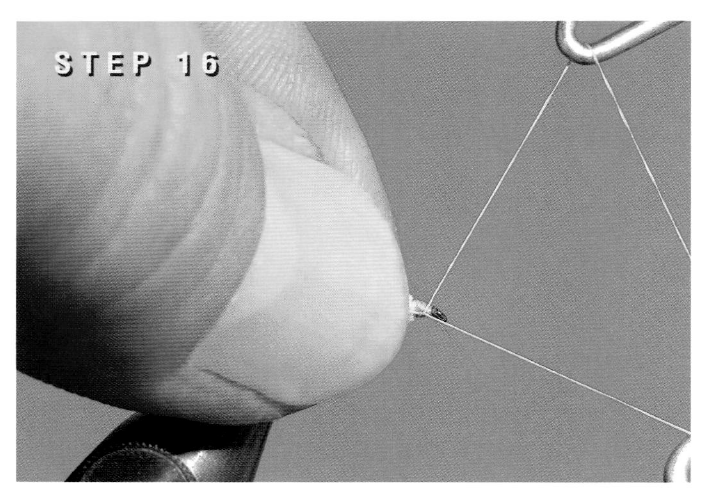

Push the hackle back and hold it with your left hand. Whip-finish behind the eye. This keeps the hackle fibers from getting trapped by the thread.

Fluff the hackle back into position and apply cement. I coat the thread head and put a sparse drop at the top of the hackle.

The finished fly.

Teal Baetis Nymph

DURING THE 2003 SEASON ON THE SNAKE RIVER, drought conditions affected our normally superb fall dry-fly fishing. Excessively high river flows were caused by irrigation draws from Jackson Lake Dam. Unfortunately, the high water was also warm from the water cooking in shallow lake flats. When the river dropped in September, it went from 5,000 cubic feet per second to 300 cfs in just over a week. We knew the fish were in the river, but standard Snake River dry flies wouldn't produce in the tough conditions.

Knowing there were probably *Baetis* nymphs in the water column, I tried one of my favorite BWO nymphs, the Teal Baetis Nymph. The fly proved effective and caught fish in pools and runs where other flies went untouched.

The fall of 2003 was gorgeous, with temperatures in the 70s and bright fall colors. Whether fishing conditions were perfect or not, we needed to be on the river. With Thibaud, my six-year-old son, in tow, we rode our bikes along the Wilson Bridge Dike and stopped at different pools to fish. Our fishing was interspersed with sand-castle building and rock-hunting episodes. Despite the Bureau of Reclamation's efforts, there was still bug activity. A few blue-winged olives could be found on the water and occasionally we saw a rise. I picked up some random fish on top, but it was pretty slow. I turned to something I rarely did on the Snake: nymph fishing. Knowing there were probably *Baetis* nymphs in the water column, I tried one of my favorite BWO nymphs, the Teal Baetis Nymph. The fly proved effective and caught fish in pools and runs where other flies went untouched. Deep nymphing produced some better cutts. And I manage to catch a few nice suckers: Rocky Mountain redfish. I had some good fishing and salvaged what could have been uneventful days.

This Teal Baetis Nymph is a variation of a soft-hackle Pheasant Tail. Pheasant Tails are fine flies and work very well during most mayfly hatches. They look buggy, have a nice variegated pattern, and the herl fibers imitate the gills on the naturals. The addition of a soft-hackle collar makes it a good imitation of an active or emerging nymph. *Baetis* are a long-lasting spring and fall hatch that trout key on. The mobile nymphs are a common food source, and they are active for some time prior to hatching. While I'd had good luck with standard Pheasant Tail patterns, I'd noticed that some *Baetis* nymphs were more gray than brown in color.

I first tied a fly with gray ruffed grouse tail-feather fibers and called it a Grouse Tail. I fished it on local waters and it also proved effective on the tailwaters of Utah's Green River. It was a deadly fly, but gray-phase grouse tails are not always readily available. In looking for a substitute, I noticed some teal flank on my bench. It was the correct color and wrapped nicely.

TEAL BAETIS NYMPH

HOOK:	Dai-Riki 135 Scud hook, sizes 14 to 20.
WEIGHT:	Silver metal or clear glass bead.
THREAD:	Olive 8/0.
ABDOMEN:	Teal flank fibers.
RIB:	Fine silver wire.
THORAX:	Olive dubbing.
HACKLE:	Dun hen or partridge.

Now I could easily buy bags of supplies at any fly shop. Mallard flank also works. During *Baetis* season, this fly can be used as a general searching pattern, but it is particularly effective when trout are keying on emerging nymphs. The trick in this situation is to fish it very shallow—six inches or less below the surface.

While I'd had good luck with Pheasant Tail patterns, I noticed that some *Baetis* nymphs were more gray than brown in color.

A dry-dropper combination is a logical choice, but the dry needs to be able to support the nymph. The nymph can be tied with more or less weight to help out. Undersized metal beads are one option. Glass will work, too. This fly can also be good during midge activity. Wood duck and dyed mallard flank can be used to create a number of other nymphs based on this basic pattern.

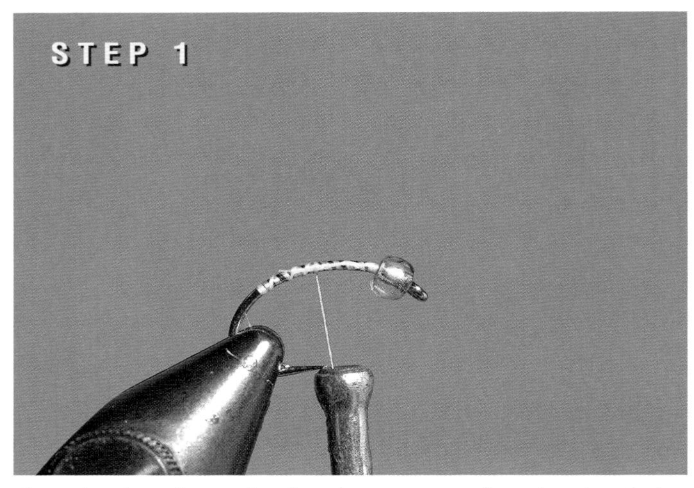

Put the bead on the hook, cement the shank of the hook, and start your thread.

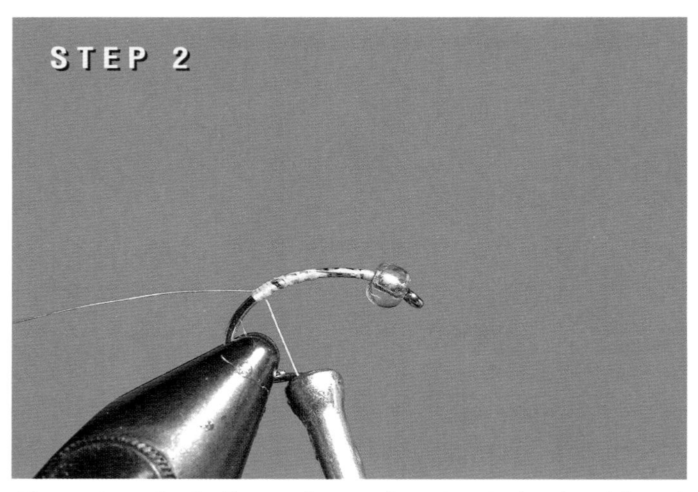

Tie a strand of silver wire to the shank. It should end up on the hook shank just above the barb.

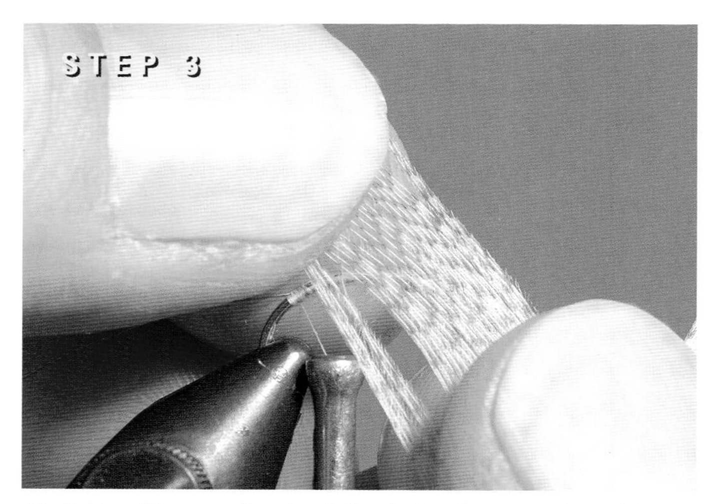

Pull the fibers of a teal flank feather to the side to align their tips. Hold the tips and pull against the grain of the fibers to pull them off the feather stem.

Tie in the tips of the teal fibers as a tail. Don't cut the butts.

Grasp the teal fibers, give them a slight twist, and wrap them up the hook shank just shy of the bead. Secure the fibers.

Reverse-rib the body with the wire and tie it off.

Dub a small thorax. This will cover the end of the wire.

Tie on a dun hen hackle and make one and a half wraps. Tie it off.

Trim the loose ends. Whip-finish and cement.

The finished fly.

Foam-Back Sparkle Dun

WE ARE FISHING SMALLER FLIES in more and more of our waters. Of course, there are certain problems in this trend. Aside from visibility, other difficulties are hooking fish and opening up hooks. As flies get below size 18, the hookup ratio seems to go down exponentially with each decrease in hook size. This problem is exacerbated by many standard dry-fly hooks because their proportions change in smaller sizes. Hooks that have an ideal shank-to-gap ratio in size 16 may have a 2X-long proportion in size 20. Unless you are careful with the body material, you can block the gap of the hook.

The advent of the new 1 mm and .5 mm foams made it practical to come up with the Foam-Back Sparkle Dun.

For many years, salmon and steelhead anglers have used oversized or stout hooks for small patterns. Trout anglers can also benefit from this strategy. Although nylon and fluorocarbon leaders keep getting stronger, the metal technology used in hooks is stagnant. We may have reached the threshold in wire strength. Basically, what has happened is we have been working with metal for thousands of years, while we have spent only 60 years with extruded nylon monofilament. In the recent past, you broke tippets; now, you're more likely to open the bend of a small hook. To address hook-strength and improve hookups, many standard patterns can be adapted to shorter-shank hooks.

Baetis are among the most common small-mayfly hatches around the world. They were the catalyst for my trying to create a good, buoyant spring-creek mayfly with a larger-gap hook. The advent of the new 1 mm and .5 mm foams made it practical to come up with the Foam-Back Sparkle Dun. Last October, I played around with some different concepts, but it took a few prototype flies to figure out a pattern that would catch fish—and looked correct to me.

The Mathews Sparkle Dun has always been one of my favorite match-the-hatch flies; I decided it would be a good idea to add a foam back. After tying a few, I met a friend, Bill App, on Wyoming's Flat Creek. I consider this one of the best public spring creeks around. Bill had found a good pod of a dozen nice cutthroats, and wanted me to try to catch them.

As we sneaked up on the pool, I noticed them rising to a sparse *Baetis* hatch. I tied one of the new flies on the end of my leader. On the second cast, I missed the biggest fish, over 20 inches. I rested them for a while and then cast to a fish along an undercut bank. He ate on the first good drift. I got a nice 18-inch fish to my feet before he broke off the fly. I rested them again, and then cast to the cutt on the inside of the corner. It took a few casts to get the drift and timing, but I was rewarded with a handsome 20-inch fish. In the end, I hooked seven of the dozen fish in the pod. I guess the new fly worked.

Another good application for this fly design is large

BAETIS FOAM-BACK SPARKLE DUN

HOOK:	Dai-Riki 125 wide-gap emerger hook, sizes 14 to 20.
THREAD:	Olive or gray Gudebrod 8/0 or 10/0.
WING:	Natural dark elk (cow) or elk dyed dark dun or black.
SHUCK:	Olive Z-Lon.
RIB:	Dun 6/0 or 8/0 thread.
BODY:	Fine olive dubbing.
BACK:	Triangular strip of olive 1 mm or .5 mm Razor Foam.

mayflies such as drakes. Sparkle Duns and Comparaduns are definitely effective imitations, but a larger hook size compromises floatation. The Foam-Back Sparkle Duns tied in drake sizes on standard-length hooks are the answer. The foam also makes it easy to tie flies with light bellies and dark backs.

On the second cast, I missed the biggest fish, over 20 inches. I rested them for a while and then cast to a fish along an undercut bank. He ate on the first good drift.

Cement the shank of the hook and create a thread base. Clean and stack a clump of elk hair. Tie in the hair behind the hook eye a distance equal to one quarter the length of the shank. Wrap in front of the wing to prop it upright; the wing should be as long as the shank of the hook.

Tie in a shank-length shuck of Z-Lon. Butt it up against the butts of the elk hair for a smoother body.

On the far side of the hook shank, tie on a doubled strand of 6/0 or 8/0 dun thread for the rib.

Dub a sparse, tapered abdomen up to the wing.

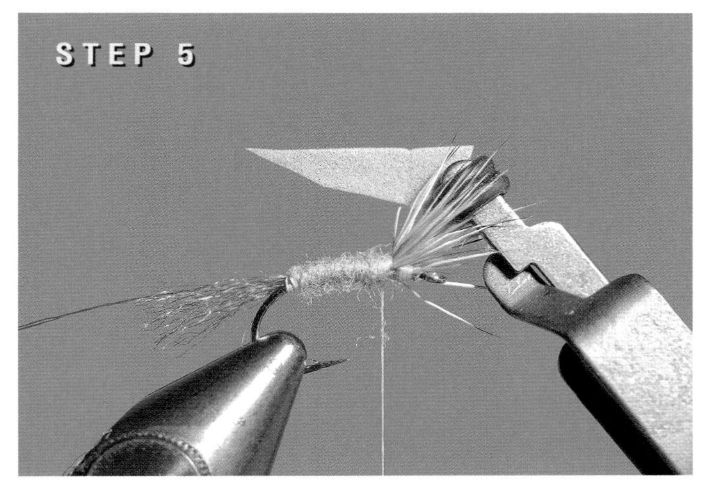

Cut a triangular piece of thin foam for the back. At the big end, it should be equal to about one third the width of the hook gap.

Secure the foam behind the hair wing with thread wraps. The tip should extend even with the back of the hook bend.

Twist the two strands of dun thread together and rib the body to secure the foam to back of the fly. Tie off the rib. Trim the tip of the foam so that it is even with the bend of the hook.

Dub in front of the wing to make the head and keep the wing upright. Make one sparse wrap behind the wing to cover the thread wraps. Whip-finish and cement.

The finished fly.

When tying small flies, I like Gudebrod 8/0 and 10/0 threads, which are finer than most other threads with this size designation; they help me tie small flies without a lot of bulk. They are also strong enough to secure the elk-hair wing. I use elk for this fly since the tips flare more easily than the tips of most deer hai, and the cream tips are visible. Consistent, straight elk also seems easier to find than deer. If you do use deer hair, make sure the tips are hollow. Once you get into the black-banded area of the tips, they aren't hollow. This makes it difficult to make the fanned-out wing and builds undesirable bulk at the tie-in.

FOAM-BACK MARCH BROWN COMPARADUN

HOOK:	Dai-Riki 320 standard dry-fly hook, size 12 or 14.
THREAD:	Brown 8/0.
WING:	Natural dark elk (cow).
TAIL:	Moose body hair.
RIB:	Dun 6/0 or 8/0 thread.
BODY:	Fine tan dubbing.
BACK:	Triangular strip of brown 1 mm closed-cell foam.

To make a split tail, flare a small bundle of moose body at the rear of the hook with thread tension and trim out the excess fibers in the center of the tail. A drop of cement reinforces the separation. The rest of the steps are the same as those for the Foam-Back Sparkle Dun.

CADDISFLIES

CADDISFLIES PROBABLY FORM THE HIGHEST BIOMASS of trout food in the Rocky Mountain region. They are available to the trout as larvae for the entire year, and good hatches of adults appear from April to October. At times, I've seen trout take caddisflies in preference to larger stoneflies. Some of the hatches, such as the famous Mother's Day caddis hatch (*Brachycentrus occidentalis*), produce huge numbers of insects—and with them a good number of winter-weary feeding trout.

Cased species, both free-living and net-spinning varieties, are found in almost every type of moving water. In some waters they provide the best dry-fly fishing. If you start flipping over rocks and looking for aquatic insects, you will be amazed at the numbers of caddisflies. Good populations of square-shaped cased caddis such as *Brachycentrus* are found in riffles and runs all year long; many other aquatic insects are there in abundance only prior to hatching. This year-round presence makes caddisflies not only important to match in the traditional sense, but also valuable as a basis for searching patterns. The fish are used to seeing them.

Glass-House Caddis

Caddisflies are vulnerable to trout at all stages of life: The larvae are standard fare all year; the emerging pupae bring trout from the depths to feed; trout sip the floating adults; and egg-laying females complete the food cycle. Mayflies may be pretty—the glamour fly of the trout stream—but caddisflies are everyday meat and potatoes.

During periods of caddisfly hatches, a basic knowledge of the Tricoptera order's lifestyles can make for more productive fishing. Throughout the year, my Glass-House Caddis works well as a cased-caddis imitation. Ultra Zugs tied in peacock, Hare's Ear, or olive colors cover most of the species whose larvae don't build cases: free-living (*Rhyacophlia*) and net-spinning (*Hydropsyche* and *Cheumatopsyche*) caddis. I like to fish caddisfly larvae slightly larger than the adults the naturals will eventually become—tie your flies on sizes 12 to 16 hooks and you'll be set for most of the Rocky Mountain caddisfly larvae.

All caddisflies change into a pupal form prior to emerging. As they prepare for the transition from pupae to adult, they are active and drift in the river's current. Fortunately, the larvae patterns work for the deep pupae. As the insects work their way to the surface, emerging-pupae patterns become very effective. The larvae patterns swung in the current or dead-drifted work well. The Ultra Zug flies pick up air bubbles in their dubbing collars, and their reflective pearl ribs imitate the air bubbles found on many of the pupae. Soft-hackles are also good choices.

The trick to swinging flies is to mend up- or downstream so that your fly moves slightly quicker than the current, with a little kick at the end of the drift. There is more of an art to this than many would think. As a caddisfly reaches the water's surface, some pupae get caught in the surface tension. The Everything Emerger imitates this stage well and can be tied in shades that match the naturals. Bodies of tan, olive, and peacock predominate.

Adult caddisflies fall into two categories: flush on the water and fluttering. To simulate freshly hatched adults sitting on the water, I use a Foam-Wing Caddis. More active naturals are best imitated by a hackled fly—the Speed Stimulator.

Caddisflies are available as adults longer than most other aquatic insects are. This creates options for more surface fishing. Evening caddisfly flights are obvious opportunities, but windy days always knock some flies in the water. Shaded coves are prime spots.

Caddisflies usually live for a few days as adults before the females return to deposit eggs. Some species lay their eggs on the surface, and others dive down to oviposit in the water. Diving caddisflies can make multiple trips in the water and rest on the surface between trips. The Speed Stimulator works well as a surface fly; dead-drifting are skittering are both good techniques. Simple soft-hackles are time-tested subsurface patterns for just this situation. The same controlled swing I fish during emergence works well here. Many times there are overlaps of emergence and egg-laying activity. Use the same flies and methods, concentrating on runs and tailouts.

Mayflies may be pretty—the glamour fly of the trout stream—but caddisflies are everyday meat and potatoes.

Glass-House Caddis

The Glass-House Caddis is an imitation of the prevalent western cased caddisfly, the *Brachycentrus*. This insect and its imitations are also commonly known as the American Grannom. The immature caddisflies grow up in identifiable dark-colored square cases, the stick houses providing cover and camouflage for the lime-colored larvae. The cases are attached to rocks. The larvae poke their heads out to feed on algae growing on the rocks or in the current. These are sometimes called peeking caddis. They aren't good swimmers, and, when dislodged, they drift in the current until they land back on the bottom or are eaten—bad for the bug, good for the trout. American Grannom are found in small mountain streams as well as big rivers. Even tailwaters such as the Missouri River have good populations. Since they can be found in quantity in riffles and runs throughout the year, they are important trout food.

This species is the cause of the Mother's Day

GLASS-HOUSE CADDIS

HOOK: Dai-Riki 060 2X-long nymph, sizes 10 to 18.

THREAD: Black 8/0.

BEADS: One black metal bead followed by an olive glass bead. If you have trouble finding olive glass beads in the correct size, green will be close enough.

RIB: Fine copper wire.

BODY/CASE: Scintilla No. 46 Peacockle dubbing.

HACKLE: Brown or dark hen.

The dubbed body of my Glass-House Caddis imitates the case of insect, while the black bead is the head and the olive glass bead is the front of the larval body. The wire rib simulates the pronounced segmentation in the stick case.

hatch. If you haven't experienced this event, you need to. Hitting the hatch takes a little luck and free scheduling. Living in the area or being voluntarily unemployed is also helpful. The hatch on the Yellowstone River near Livingston is nothing short of amazing; good hatches also take place on the lower Madison. The bugs are there in quantity and the feeding fish are, too. You'll see rafts of adults in back eddies. Inside corners are littered with the dark-colored tent-winged flies. In the mornings prior to emergence or egg laying, dry-fly patterns are a random proposition. However, a Glass-House works very well as the pupae become active and are loosely drifting in the current. Later, when the adults come in contact with the water, surface fishing starts. This event is always a mad race between spring runoff and the hatch. You want it warm enough for the bugs to start, but no so warm that the snow melts.

Having seen *Brachycentrus* in most the waters I fished, I wanted a good imitation of the dark-cased caddisfly. I found that most of the existing patterns were too light in color for this particular insect. While fishing with Dubs Horgan of Kidd, Montana, I learned about his Chairman fly. He used the pattern to fool fish for himself and clients on his home river, the Beaverhead. He called it the Chairman because everyone listens to the chairman. His fly was tied entirely of dubbing. I took this and added the double-bead set-up, a wire rib, and a soft hackle. I then had the fly I needed.

The dubbed body of my Glass-House Caddis imitates the case of the insect, while the black bead is the head and the olive glass bead is the front of the larval body. The wire rib simulates the pronounced segmentation in the stick case. The double-bead arrangement gets the fly down to the trout's level, and the glass bead provides just enough flash to catch their attention. The soft hackle is an exaggeration of the natural's legs. It also gives motion to the fly. Although the fly was designed to imitate the cased larva, it is close enough in coloration and size to be taken as a pupa. Letting it swing at the end of a drift can entice some aggressive takes.

The Glass-House Caddis quickly gathered miles and fish, with good results on the Yellowstone, Gallatin, Madison, Henry's Fork, Missouri, and even the Guadalupe in Texas. Colorado anglers have also reported good results. With the success of the original, I have added a lighter-colored Glass-House with a tan case and amber glass bead. This version is good for species (*Glossosoma* and *Dicosmoecus*) that make their cases of sand or pebbles.

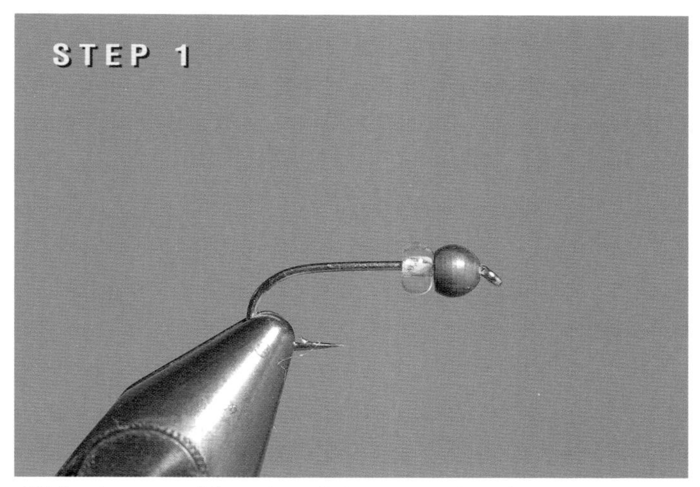

Slide the metal bead and the glass bead on the shank of the hook.

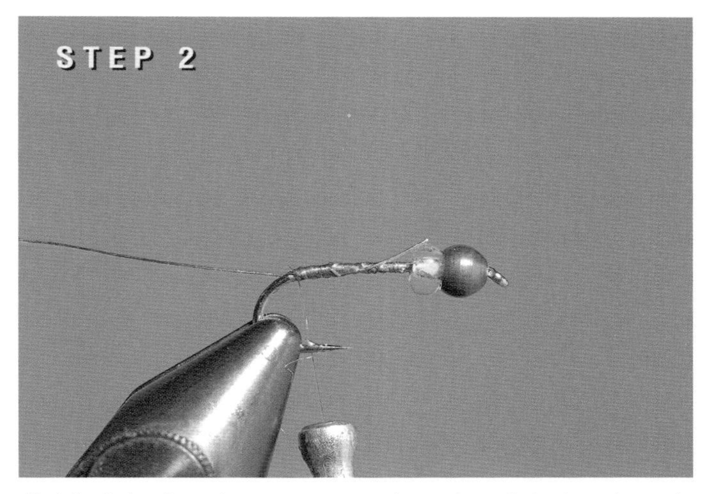

Behind the beads, start your thread and tie in a length of copper wire.

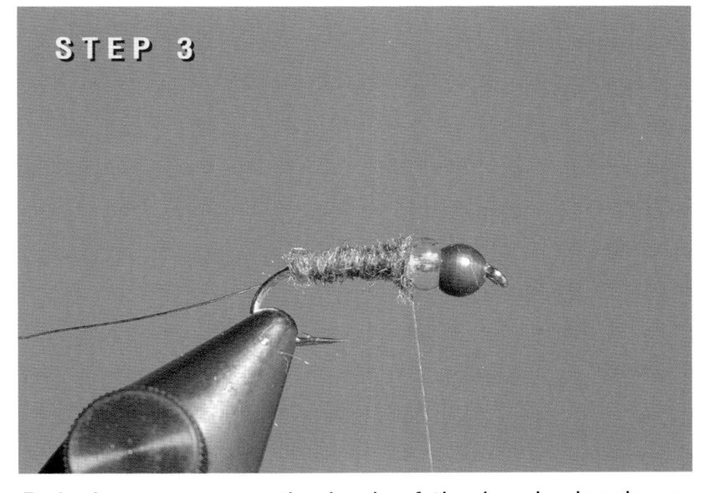

Dub the case up to the back of the beads, leaving a very small gap between the dubbing and the glass bead.

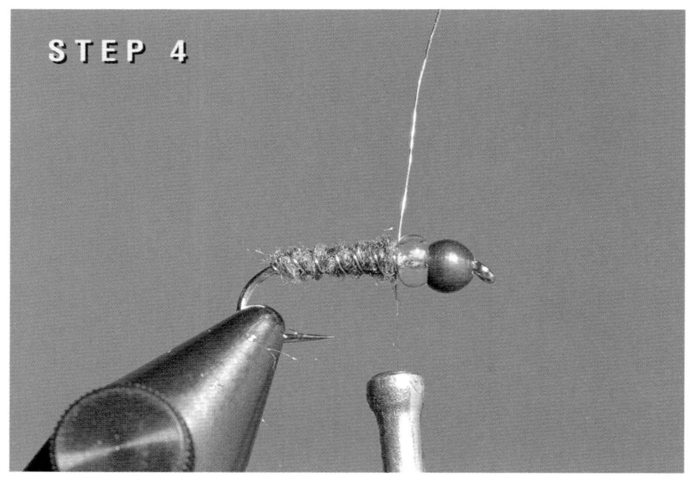

Reverse-rib the dubbing with the copper wire. When you get to the front, make a couple of firm wraps with the wire so it sinks in between the bead and dubbing.

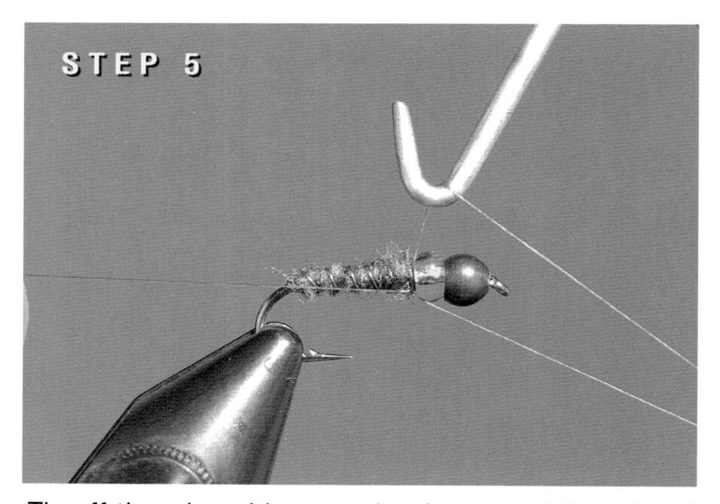

Tie off the wire with a couple of wraps of thread and a whip finish. Cement.

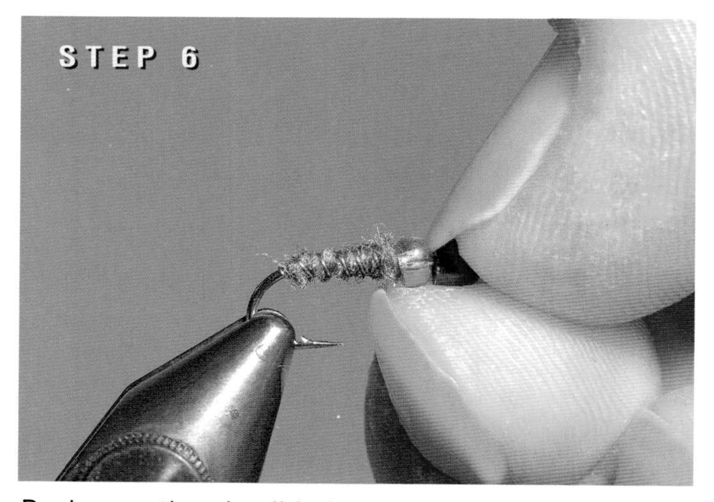

Push your thumbnail in between the glass and metal beads. This makes a small void, and pushes the end of the wire under the dubbing.

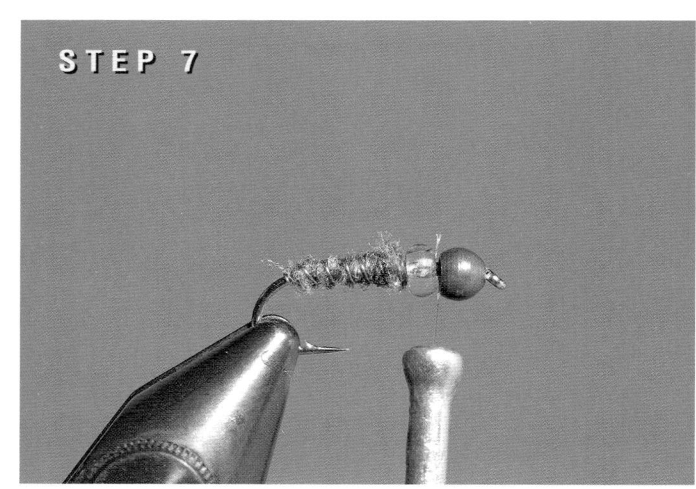

Start your thread between the beads. Start the thread as usual and then twist the tag end around the main thread a few times and wrap—this makes sure the thread is connected and secure.

Tie in the soft hackle and make about one and a half wraps. The hackle fibers should be equal to about two hook gaps. Tie the hackle off, whip-finish, and cement.

The finished fly.

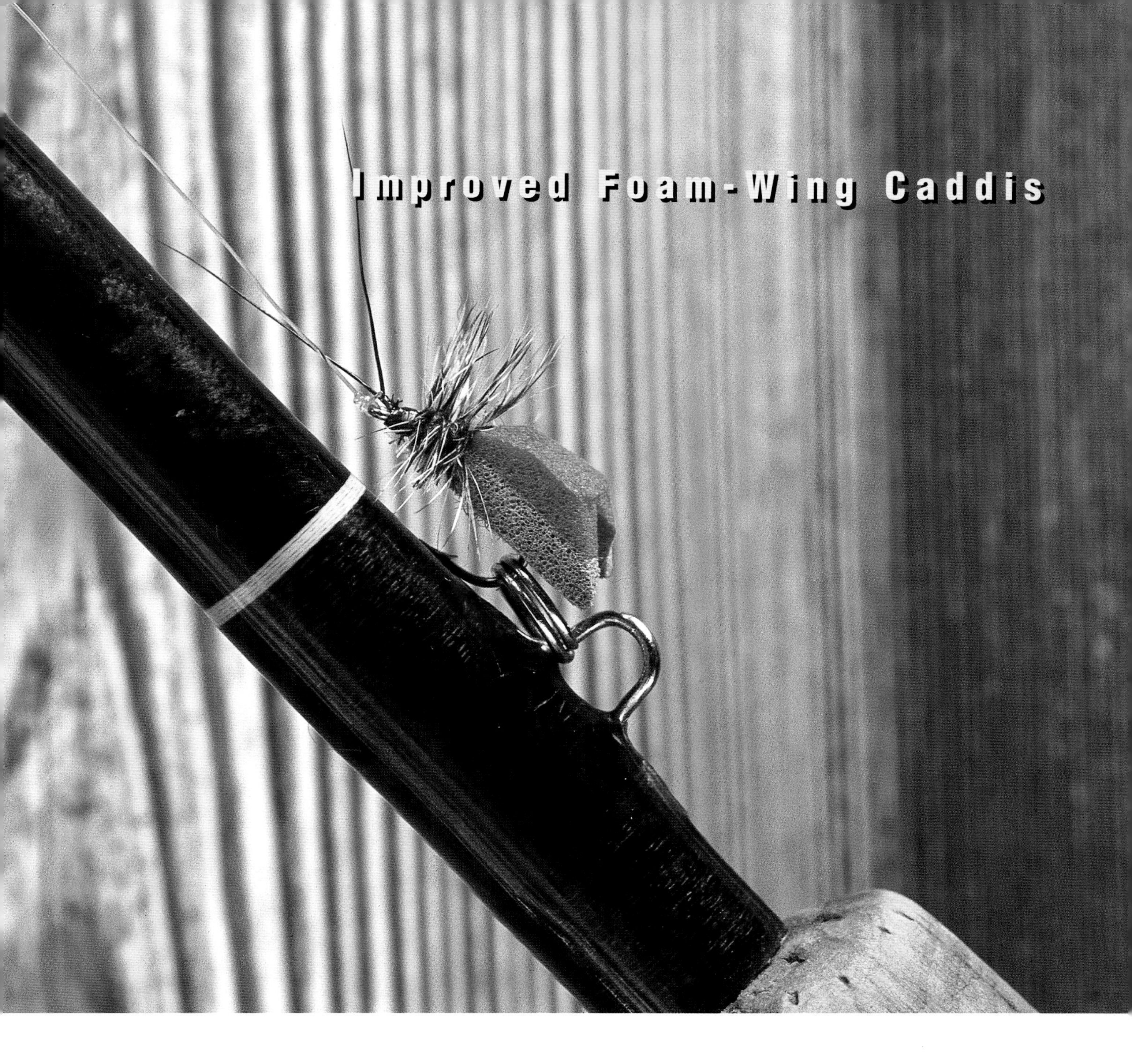

Improved Foam-Wing Caddis

FOR FISHING DURING CADDISFLY HATCHES, I like to have two styles of adults: a flush-floating imitative fly and a bushy fly for simulating a fluttering insect. The Foam-Wing Caddis is my favorite imitative adult caddis.

The Foam-Wing Caddis imitates an adult drifting after emergence, a female resting between laying eggs, or a spent insect. It has proved itself on tough waters such as the Henry's Fork and Firehole, and in a size 16 or 18 it works great for early season dark caddis. It is basically a synthetic Goddard Caddis—a fly people love to fish but hate to tie. With a buoyant foam wing, it has an advantage over some other low-floaters that perform in smooth current but not so well in heavier currents. It is a caddisfly adult for all water types.

The original pattern used 1/8-inch Evasote foam for the wing; and I threaded the foam onto the hook. I put a drop of bright paint on the top of the wing to serve as an indicator. This style of foam can still be a viable option if you don't want to glue foam sheets. With the advent of the more durable 2 mm craft foams, which come in numerous colors, I have switched to laminated double layers of this product. An added bonus of the craft foam is that seems to glue better. By using bright foam on the top, and a foam color that matches the insect on the bottom, both angler and fish get the desired view. New, thin foams can be used for a smaller indicator top. Wrightway Sports has recently started producing pre-made wings for my Foam-Wing Caddis.

In the sequential tying photos, you'll see that I used a very bright indicator, but darker colors such as tan or black provide decent visibility and are closer in color to the natural.

A spray contact adhesive cement works well for laminating sheets of foam. A readily available product is 3M's Super 77 Adhesive, which can be found in hardware stores; it's distributed to fly shops by Wapsi. Spray the inside of two large foam sheets, let the glue set, and then press the sheets together. Small sections can be put together with super glue.

Prepping wings speeds up the tying process. An easy way to make a bunch of wings is to cut a strip of foam slightly longer than the wing and then cut the foam in a zig zag. You can also cut wings out of pre-made two-tone Chernobyl bodies. This fly can be tied in other colors to match local insects. The hackle on this fly is more for balance and to suggest legs than it is for flotation. On larger flies, rubber legs can be used in place of the hackle. The body material is fine vernille. This is the San Juan worm material in an extra-small size. Micro Dub, New Dubb, and Micro Body are common brands. A very fine yarn or twisted Antron fibers also works.

IMPROVED FOAM-WING CADDIS

HOOK:	Dai-Riki 125 light-wire emerger, sizes 12 to 18.
THREAD:	Black Gudebrod 8/0 on smaller sizes and UNI 8/0 on larger sizes.
BELLY:	Olive or black fine vernille.
WING:	A double layer of craft foam cut to shape.
THORAX:	Scintilla No. 46 Peacockle dubbing.
HACKLE:	Grizzly dyed dun; the fibers should be one and a half to two gap-widths in length.
ANTENNAE:	Moose body hair.

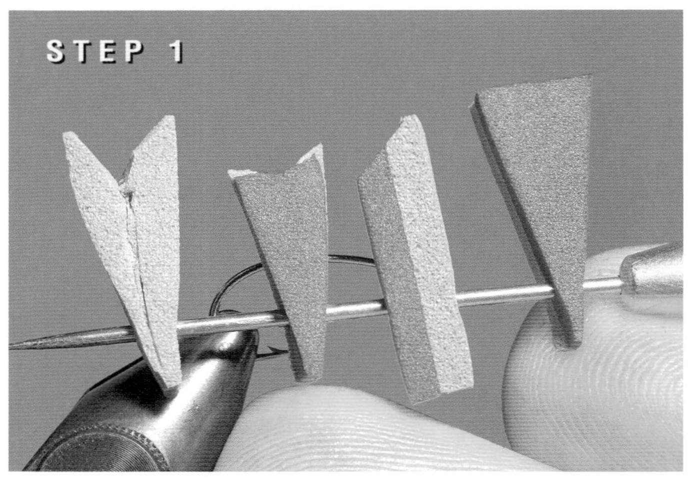

Cut the wing to shape. The first cut is a triangle equal to about one and a half lengths of the hook shank. Next, notch the back of wing to make a V, and then taper the back to make it look like a caddisfly wing. Gently slit the bottom with scissors or a razor knife. Try not to cut through the wing. The sequence on the bodkin goes right to left.

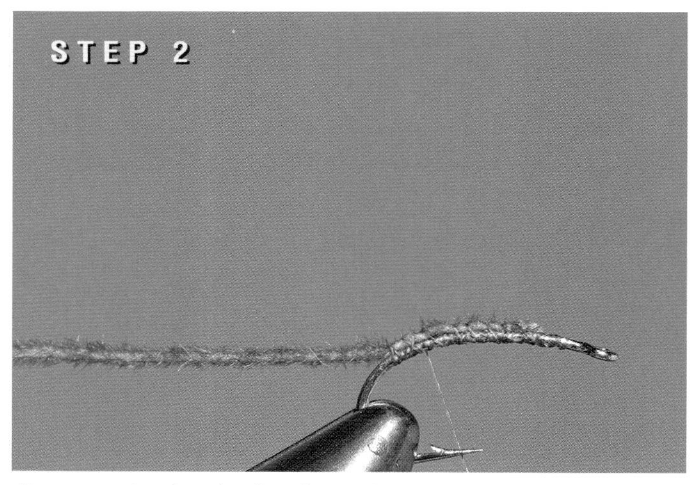

Cement the hook shank, make a thread base, and tie in a strand of Micro Chenille along the top of the shank, back down the bend. (The material on the shank acts as a glue base, and the curve of the hook acts like a popper-hook kink to keep the foam from twisting.)

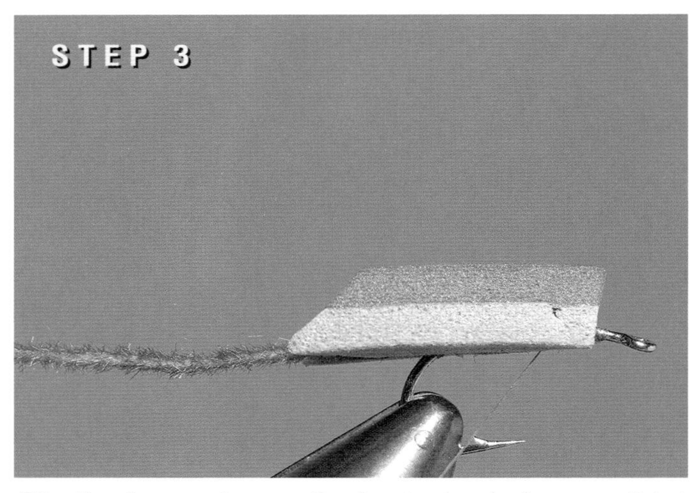

Slip the foam wing on the hook shank. Leave a third of a shank of bare hook behind hook eye. The wing should extend half a shank past the bend. Snip some of the front of wing if necessary—I usually taper the front of the wing at this point.

Secure the front of the wing with thread. Make a few soft wraps and then add thread pressure.

Use a bodkin or toothpick to lightly coat the slit in the underside of the wing with super glue, and then push the wing down to secure it to the hook. Pinch the sides of foam to help secure it.

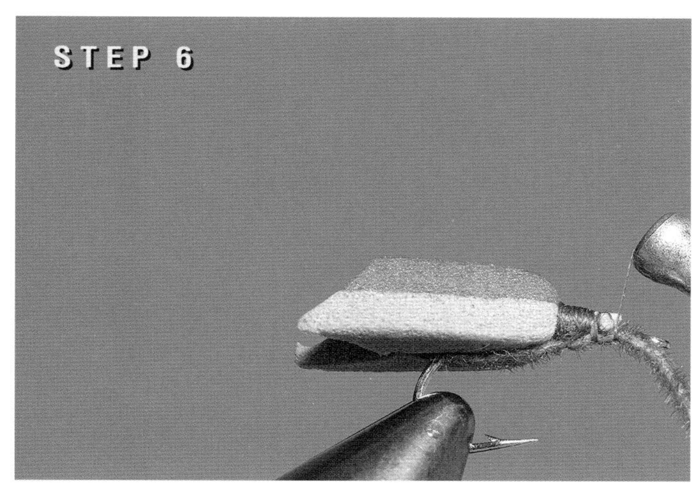

Pull the vernille forward to make the belly and tie it off.

Tie in the antennae and the hackle. The antennae will be a shank and a half long, and the hackle fibers one and half gaps.

Dub the thorax. Leave room to tie off the hackle.

Palmer the hackle through the thorax.

Tie off the hackle and whip-finish.

Trim the hackle on the bottom of the fly so that it's flush with the belly.

The finished fly.

Parachute Foam-Wing Caddis

I sometimes tie the Foam-Wing Caddis as a parachute. A parachute pattern doesn't need an indicator on the foam wing because the post serves as an indicator. To tie a parachute version, begin with steps 1 through 6 above, and then proceed as follows.

Take a piece of Antron or poly yarn and secure the center of it on the thorax.

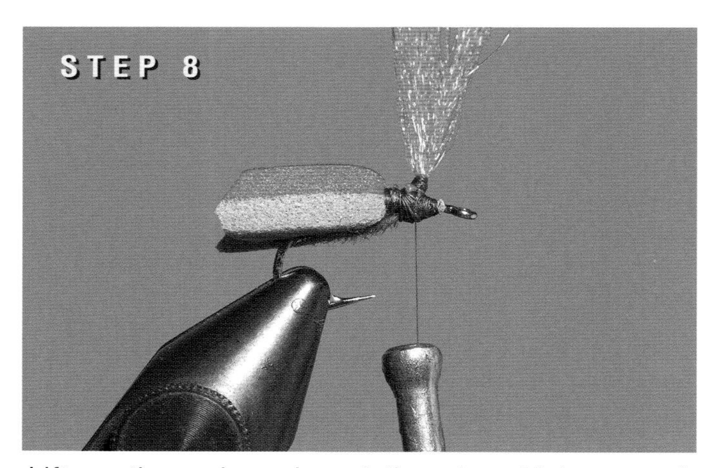

Lift up the ends and post the wing. Make enough wraps to create a firm base for the hackle and put a drop of glue at the base.

Tie in a hackle and dub the thorax.

Wrap the hackle parachute style, tie it off, and cement.

The finished fly.

Speed Stimulator

MY SPEED STIMULATOR IS A COMBINATION of the standard Elk Hair Caddis and the Stimulator. It isn't anything revolutionary, but it fills the niche in my fly box for a bushy, buoyant caddisfly or small stonefly. This style of fly imitates a fluttering caddis or egg-laying stone; it provides visibility and flotation on the choppy water associated with these insects. The hackle leaves a footprint that looks like a moving insect.

I've had the chance to fish with Randall Kaufmann and talk about flies with him. One time we talked about Al Troth's original Elk Hair Caddis and his Stimulator. We both agreed the Elk Hair Caddis is a great fly, but felt that proportionately it needed more bulk in the front of the fly to look right to us. Randall tied his Stimulator to address this desire.

The Stimulator is an effective fly and has caught plenty of fish for me. However, it has a few more steps and takes more time to tie than I like. Another problem with the standard Stimulator tie is that in small sizes the combination of the light-wire, long-shank hook (TMC 200 or Dai-Riki 270) and heavy hackles sometimes keeps the fish from coming in contact with the hook point, leading to missed strikes.

I like this hook-and-fly combination in flies over size 12, but not in smaller configurations. In addition, the commonly fished caddis sizes of 12 to 16, when tied on a TMC 200, require a hook three sizes smaller for the same shank-length. This can be a problem with larger fish, in heavy currents, and with the growing strengths of modern tippets, especially when barbarians like me have been known to fish 4X or even 3X with these patterns. A standard dry-fly hook takes care of both the strength and hookup requirements.

Dead-drifting the Speed Stimulator works well; twitching and skittering it are other effective methods. I have had some great evening caddisfly fishing on the long runs of the Yellowstone River with this fly. Skittering the fly can provoke some explosive takes. Sometimes you don't get the fish, but the visuals are well worth the misses. The buoyant nature of this fly makes it a good strike indicator, and early in a caddis hatch a Glass-House Caddis or Ultra Zug suspended below it does a good job of imitating emerging pupae. Elk hair, light or dark, is standard for this fly, but I'll

SPEED STIMULATOR

HOOK:	Dai-Riki 320 standard dry-fly, sizes 10 to 18.
THREAD:	Gray 8/0.
BODY HACKLE:	Dyed-dun grizzly.
ABDOMEN:	Synthetic hare's-ear dubbing.
WING:	Snowshoe-hare foot hair.
THORAX:	Synthetic hare's-ear dubbing.
HACKLE:	Dyed-dun grizzly.

use another great caddisfly wing material on this fly: snowshoe-hare foot hair. Snowshoe hare looks buggy and is virtually unsinkable. Good body colors are hare's ear, peacock, olive, and tan. I like a grizzly or dyed-grizzly hackle. The long genetic hackles now available make this fly possible. To balance the fly, the hackle is wrapped facing back on the abdomen and facing forward on the thorax.

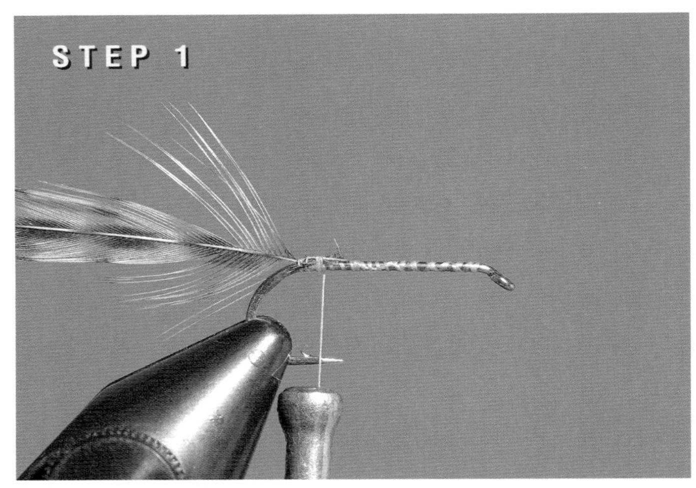

Cement the hook shank and lay down a thread base. Tie in a grizzly saddle hackle with the convex or shiny side facing forward. The fibers should be equal to one or one and a half gaps of the hook.

Dub the abdomen on the rear two thirds of the hook shank.

Palmer the hackle over the abdomen and tie it off. Don't cut the excess hackle off—it will be the thorax hackle.

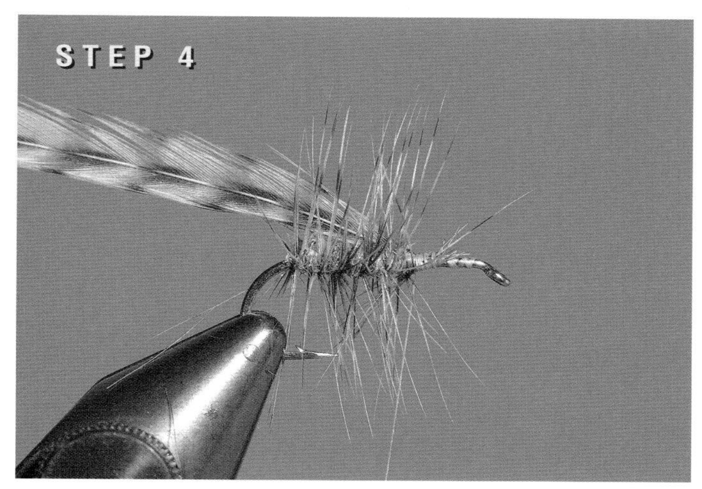

Pull the hackle forward and then lash it back with your thread so that the concave (dull side) faces forward.

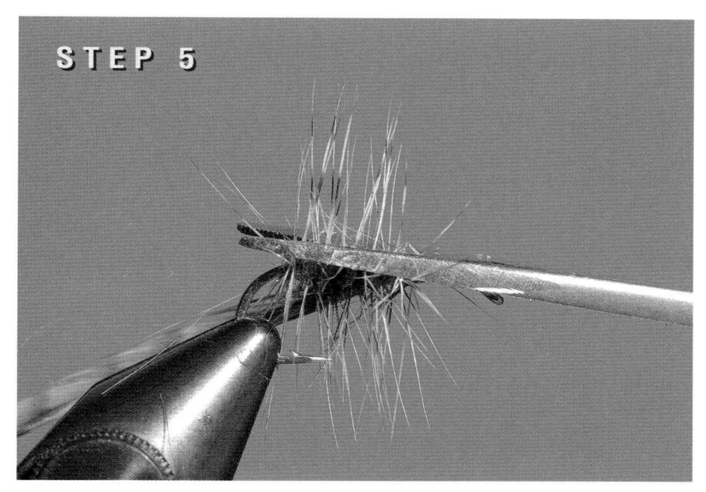

Trim the hackle fibers on top of the hook shank. This keeps them from interfering with the wing.

Tie in a wing of snowshoe hare. The tips should extend a third a shank-length past the bend of the hook.

Dub the thorax. It will be a little thicker than the abdomen.

Densely palmer the hackle through the thorax, tie it off, whip-finish, and cement. The thorax hackle should be heavier than the body hackle.

The finished fly.

CHAPTER 4

STONEFLIES

MY HOME WATERS ARE FAMOUS FOR THEIR STONEFLY HATCHES. Nowhere else thrives such variety and abundance of species belonging to the order Plecoptera. Some form of stonefly can be found emerging as early as February right through to October. Throughout their lives, stoneflies flirt with trout disaster. The nymphs of most species expose themselves as they crawl from the shallows to streamside vegetation and rocks. After shedding their nymphal skins, they change into adults. The adults are clumsy fliers and frequently get blown onto the water. Sometimes trout can be found waiting for them to drop. Egg-laying activity also brings them in contact with the water and fish.

Pteronarcys californica, commonly called salmonfly in the Rockies, is the most famous of the stoneflies. It attracts the most attention from anglers. Exact timing of emergences can be difficult to predict, and many devoted fly fishers spend lifetimes trying to intercept them. When you hit it right, though, it is amazing. The Madison, Big Hole, Yellowstone, and South Fork of the Snake are host to the annual late-spring spectacle.

Light Stone Biot Bug

Nowhere else thrives such variety and abundance of species belonging to the order *Plecoptera*. Some form of stonefly can be found emerging as early as February right through to October.

The golden stonefly complex of insects (Perlidae) hatches from April to early October. Locally they may be referred to as willowflies or plain old trout flies. Some hatch prior to runoff. Although dry-fly fishing can't be relied on, nymphs are deadly. The best golden activity is in July. In most rivers, emergence begins in late May or early June—about the same time as the riotous salmonflies take flight—but lasts much longer than the hatch of their beefy relatives. Generally, we don't see large quantities of goldens on the water, but the trout are always ready for a meal of this size. About the time the goldens taper off, their cousins, the brown stones, (*Claassenia*) start appearing. The males of the species feature only half a wing; when caught on the water they run. This may account for the effectiveness of rubber-leg patterns and heavily hackled flies twitched on the surface. The males emerge first and lie in wait for the female's nocturnal emergence, similar to their human counterparts. Just trade a gravel bar for the cocktail lounge.

Thanks to the crawl-out emergence of larger stoneflies, nymph fishing during hatches is a reliable approach. At times, it may take a while for fish to key on adults, and common nocturnal emergences encourage trout to cruise in the shallows looking for nourishing morsels each morning. This is when twitching Yuk Bugs off the bank is most effective. The best fishing happens around the tail end of runoff. The bugs crawl out on the willows and the flooded willows provide cover for the fish. If you're losing flies on the branches, you're probably fishing correctly.

A good number of anglers associate stoneflies only with salmonflies, golden stones, and large rivers. Don't be fooled. Don't allow the excitement caused by the size and splash of the big bugs to divert your attention from the plentiful smaller species. Although larger stoneflies are found predominantly in bigger waters, the smaller stoneflies are found throughout the Rockies in small trickles to medium-size creeks to full-sized rivers. You'll find hatches of smaller stoneflies all through trout season. They typically last from three to ten weeks. Their longevity makes them important—their sustained presence on many excellent streams bridges times when other aquatic insects aren't available.

Tiny wintertime black and brown stoneflies that hatch by crawling up snowbanks frequently get overlooked because their size and coloration is similar to those of the midges visible at the same time. Fortunately, some midge patterns do double duty as suitable imitations. Their height of activity is in February and March.

"Sally" is a generic name for many small, light-colored stoneflies of summer. July is peak season, but they are around earlier and later. Their body colors are shades of yellow, light green, and tan. They range in size from 1/3 of an inch to more than 3/4 of an inch. The exact color, genus, and species vary widely; exact identification is probably more important to a clinical entomologist than to the average angler. Habits and imitations are similar. Important exceptions are the *Isoperla* stoneflies, sometimes referred to as Mormon Girls, which emerge by both the typical crawling method and by drifting to the surface like mayflies. A yellowish body with a bright-red or orange butt makes them easy to identify.

If you expect to encounter adult stoneflies, carry both a low-floating pattern and a bushy, high-floating pattern. The fly that rides lower imitates an adult stuck on the water—one that was blown off a bush or a female that became stuck when ovipositing. The high floater imitates a female fluttering or either sex trying to stay clear of the water. The hackle can also act as a weedguard when fishing along bank vegetation.

LIGHT STONE BIOT BUG

HOOK:	Dai-Riki 060 1X-heavy, 1X-long nymph hook, sizes 10 to 16.
THREAD:	Rusty-brown 8/0.
WEIGHT:	Copper bead of appropriate size.
RIB:	Fine copper wire.
ABDOMEN:	Yellow Wing Fiber or Antron.
SIDES/TAILS:	Brown biots.
THORAX:	Hare's ear or tan synthetic dubbing.
HACKLE:	Brown hen hackle or partridge.

Light-Stone Biot Bug

My fascination with Yellow Sallies started with my first fly-caught fish. The pattern that fooled that Boy Scout-camp rainbow was a Mormon Girl wet fly. I have to admit that I didn't know what the fly imitated. But I devoured all the fly-fishing books and magazines that I could get my 12-year-old hands on, and discovered the fly imitated small yellow stoneflies called the Yellow Sally: *Isoperla mormona* and *quinquepunctata*

Mormon Girl is a common nickname that old-timers in the West called this insect. It was a standard wet and dry fly in my home state of Utah. This name derives from the brightly colored dresses popular among young Mormon women in the early part of the last century. Simple, colorful imitations were fished effectively by my friends' fathers and grandfathers, who didn't realize how handicapped they were with level lines and automatic reels. The impressive trout they routinely caught didn't mind their unimpressive equipment.

My Biot Bug nymphs originated as an imitation of *Isoperla* stonefly nymphs when, in 1987, Jack Dennis assigned me the entomology section for a beginners' fly-fishing school. While seining nymphs on lower Flat Creek, I noticed most of the small stonefly nymphs had brown sides with a pronounced yellow racing-stripe down the back. With Dan Abrams's help, I figured out they were yellow Sally nymphs. I knew what the adults looked like; now I had an exact visual image of the nymph to imitate.

I believe an important aspect of imitation is to look at simple but obvious features—the defined vertical line seemed worthy of imitation. I first tied a Pheasant Tail with a strand of yellow floss down the back, but I found out the color of the floss changed too much when wet. I decided to try an entirely different approach: I switched to heavy gold wire for the body and secured brown biots down the sides with a reverse-wrap of the wire rib.

This fly had the right look. Eventually, I changed the body to a Wing Fiber or Antron center. I used copper wire for the rib and added a soft hackle. These materials looked more like the natural and didn't change color when wet. The copper wire rib across the body is also similar to the lateral patterns in many stonefly nymphs. My early versions were tied as unweighted soft-hackles, which make excellent emergers and shallow-water nymphs. Bead heads came on the scene shortly after I created the fly—they were a logical way to weight the fly and maintain the slim profile.

Prior to emerging, stonefly nymphs migrate toward shore. Their increase in mobility makes them vulnerable to predation. As they move from subsurface structure, they become more visible and risk being dislodged. This is a wonderful time to fish nymphs. Dead-drifting flies with an occasional twitch and swinging flies in the current are effective ways of imitating this activity. The best method varies from day to day.

There is some dispute over the emergence style of Sallies. In most cases, stonefly nymphs crawl out on bankside structure and then change into adults. However, I've seen what appears to be a mayfly-type drift emergence of stoneflies. On Idaho's South Fork of the Snake, I have witnessed what looked like *Isoperla* nymphs changing into adults at the water's surface. Most of this activity happens in shallow riffles or runs. It's possible that the "emergers" are cripples, prematurely changing into adults, or dislodged nymphs giving their best shot at survival and propagation. Whatever it is—these flies work.

With the success of the Biot Bug design, I added more colors to cover other small stonefly species. Along with the original pattern, the Dark-Stone Biot Bug and the Pheasant Tail Biot Bug cover the color range of most small western stoneflies. These flies consistently fool trout around the country, along with the occasional steelhead.

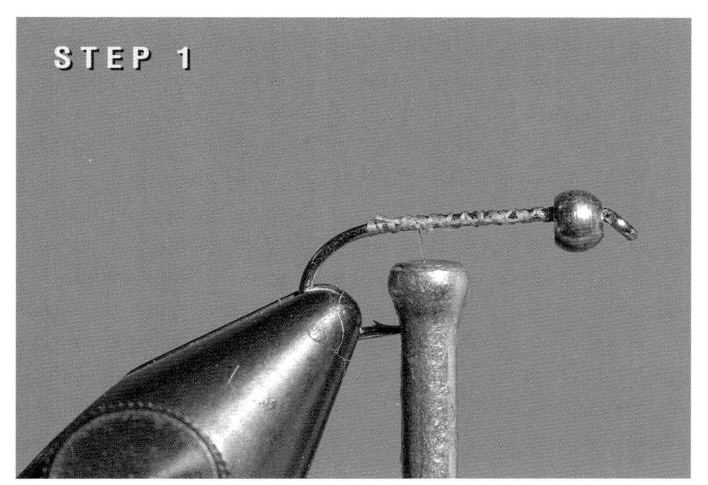

Slide the bead onto the shank of the hook. Cement the hook shank and start the tying thread.

Tie in the copper wire and Wing Fiber on top of the shank and wrap the thread back to the bend—this will help keep the body uniform in diameter.

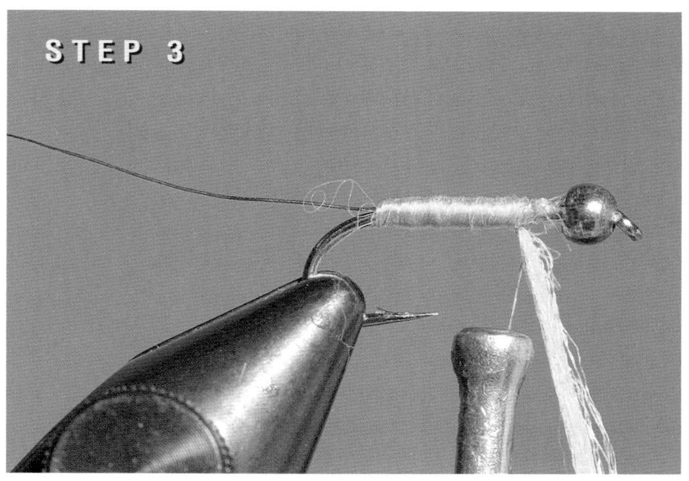

Wrap the Wing Fiber over the rear two thirds of the hook shank and tie itoff. This makes a floss-like body.

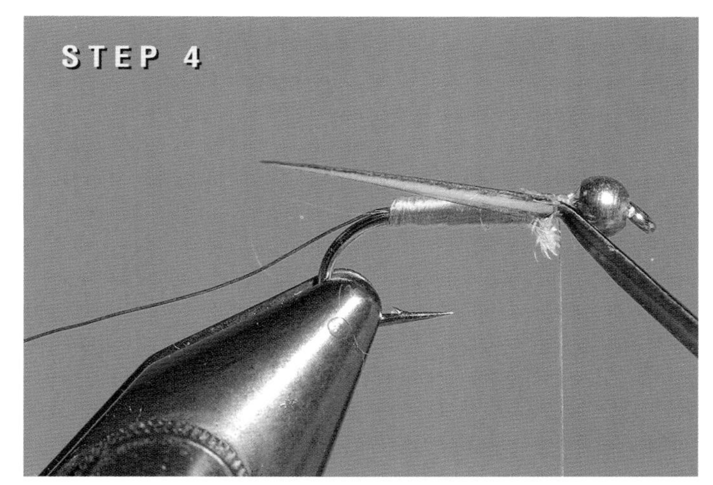

Tie in a biot on the near side. The curvature should face out and the tail should extend two thirds the length of the shank past the bend of the hook.

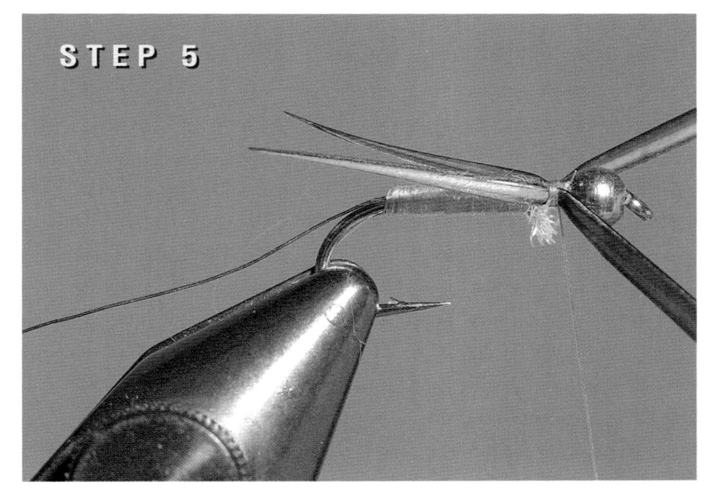

Repeat this on the far side. Push the biot tips together to make sure they are even in length. If not, gently pull on the butts until they align.

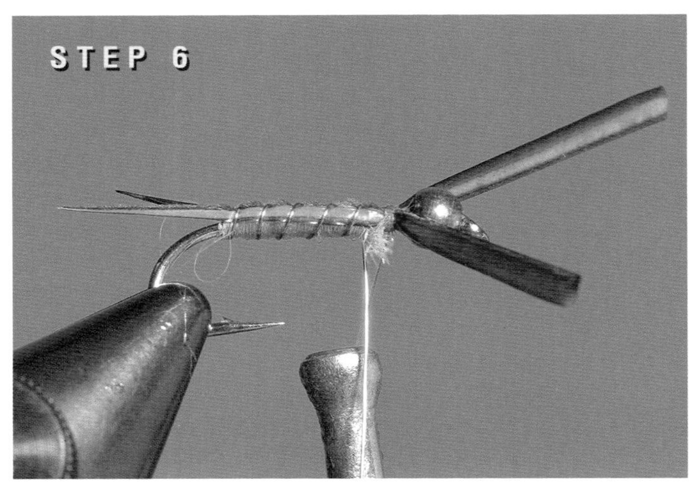

Make a wrap with the copper wire three-quarters around the hook shank and body. Next, hold the near biot against the body as you secure it with the wire. Continue wrapping over and catch the far biot. Rib the biots and body up to the bead. Tie off and cut the wire.

Dub over the wire butt to make a thorax. It will be the size of the bead.

Tie in a soft hackle and make one or two wraps, tie off, and whip finish. The hackle should be equal to two hook gaps in length.

The Finished Fly.

DARK-STONE BIOT BUG

HOOK:	Dai Riki 060 1X-long nymph, sizes 10 to 18.
THREAD:	Black 8/0.
WEIGHT:	Black bead.
RIB:	Silver wire.
BODY:	Black Antron or Wing Fiber.
SIDES/TAILS:	Dark brown biots.
THORAX:	Black dubbing.
HACKLE:	Black hen.

PHEASANT TAIL BIOT BUG

HOOK:	Dai Riki 060 1X-long nymph, sizes 10 to 18.
THREAD:	Rusty-brown 8/0.
WEIGHT:	Copper bead.
BODY:	Pheasant-tail fibers.
SIDES/TAILS:	Dark brown biots.
THORAX:	Peacock Angel Hair dubbing.
HACKLE:	Brown hen.

Sally Stone

YELLOW SALLIES ARE A SIGNIFICANT WESTERN SUMMER HATCH. While some anglers overlook them, the trout certainly don't. At times, I've seen trout take Sallies in preference to salmonflies, golden stones, *and* pale morning duns. Whether they take them as a main course or an after-dinner mint, the fact is trout eat these insects. They are widespread throughout the topography and elevation of the Rockies regions, in waters of all sizes. Sallies are plentiful in large rivers such as the Yellowstone and the Snake, in high-country trickles, and in everything between. Even tailwaters contain these insects, if they are indigenous to the original river or its tributaries. Good examples of tailwater Sally hatches are Montana's Missouri and Beaverhead, and both forks of the Snake River in Idaho.

Sallies are plentiful in large rivers such as the Yellowstone and the Snake along with high-country trickles and in everything in between. Even tailwaters contain these insects.

Adult Sallies are late-spring and summer insects. The timing of this season varies depending on latitude and altitude. Thanks to the differences of temperatures at various elevations, anglers can follow insect activity upstream and follow the peak of the hatch. In the West, consistent water temperatures of around 50 degrees Fahrenheit signal the start of activity. A variety of factors can stall or precipitate the timing of the hatches. Cold weather slows things down; a sunny, hot spell accelerates activity. Tributaries, springs, and dams can also affect water temperature and ignite hatches simultaneously at different elevations.

Hatches also occur during different times of day. Water and air temperatures are important in the timing. Evening and afternoon emergences are common in many waters, and nocturnal movement may be a survival trait. In the cool climate of higher elevations or in northern latitudes, midday hatches can be predominant. Many of the Sallies in the Rockies seem to prefer the heat of the day—May, June, and July morning water temperatures can be cool. In addition, shaded waters such as headwater streams are less susceptible to radiant heat and don't warm as quickly. Simple observation will help you determine when you should focus your fishing.

The *Isoperla* stoneflies commonly called Mormon Girls have bright-red butts, which are visible form a distance. Many anglers mistake this for an egg sac, but it is just body coloration found on both males and females. I believe this is an important feature to imitate. I've seen plenty of days when flies with a red tag outfished others.

The similar profile of stonefly nymphs and adults is interesting. While most other aquatic insects change radically from nymph to adult, stoneflies retain the same essential shape. The adult shape resembles a nymph with wings. Sometimes concepts are too close for us to easily grasp: In 2000, I finally added a dry-fly version of the Biot Bug. It has a dubbed body, pearl lure-tape wings, a palmered hackle though the thorax, and a foam indicator. Alex Nixon and I first fished it

SALLY STONE

HOOK:	Dai-Riki 270 3X-long natural-bend hook, sizes 10 to 16.
THREAD:	Light Cahill 8/0.
ANTENNAE:	Light olive biots.
RIB:	Fine copper wire.
ABDOMEN:	Red 2 mm foam and pale yellow dubbing.
SIDES/TAILS:	Olive biots.
WING:	Pearl lure tape stuck to a strip of plastic bag.
INDICATOR:	Lime foam.
HACKLE:	Golden badger or light ginger trimmed on the bottom.
THORAX:	Pale yellow dubbing.

during the stonefly smorgasbord of early July. We dropped the boat in at Tom Miner Bridge, equipped with a good supply of flies and beer and Alex's sushi-eating dog, Amos. (Watch where you release those fish!) We were into fish immediately. Along deep willow and rock banks we fished salmonflies and goldens, but as we reached riffles and tailouts, the trout wanted Sallies. We ended up putting a golden on the end and a Sally Stone in front. The rainbows in the shallows snarfed down the Sally Stone; often the takes were more aggressive than those to the larger flies. We had a couple of banner days on the upper Yellowstone with a good mix of healthy cutts, browns, and 'bows.

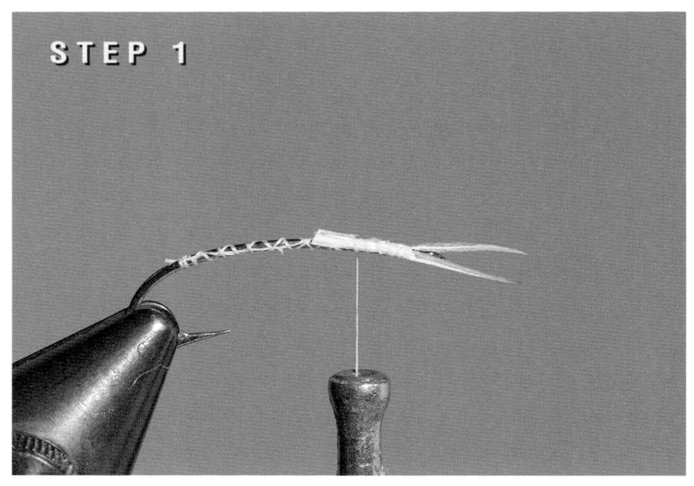

Cement the hook shank and start the thread. Tie in the antennae. The biots should be half a shank length past the eye of the hook.

The similar profile of stonefly nymphs and adults is interesting. While most other aquatic insects change radically from nymph to adult, stoneflies retain the same essential shape.

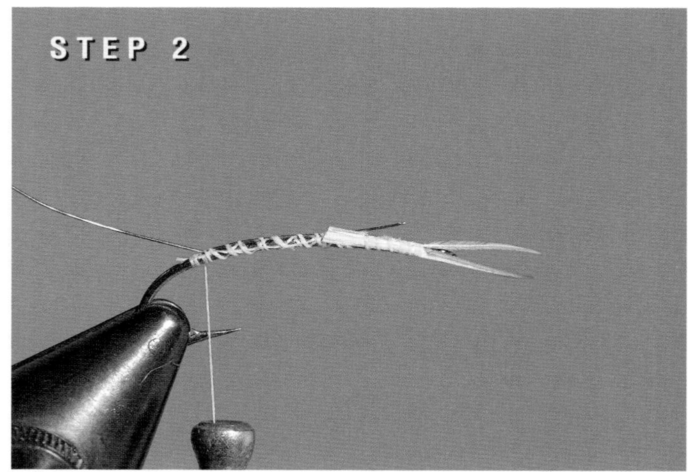

Tie in the wire rib. Go down the hook shank to the point above the barb.

This fly can be tied in various colors. Amber imitates a number of stoneflies. Olive or green versions cover lime Sallies. And black is good for winter stones. The red butt can be eliminated. Foam can be used for the bodies on larger sizes, and feather wings are optional in place of the plastic.

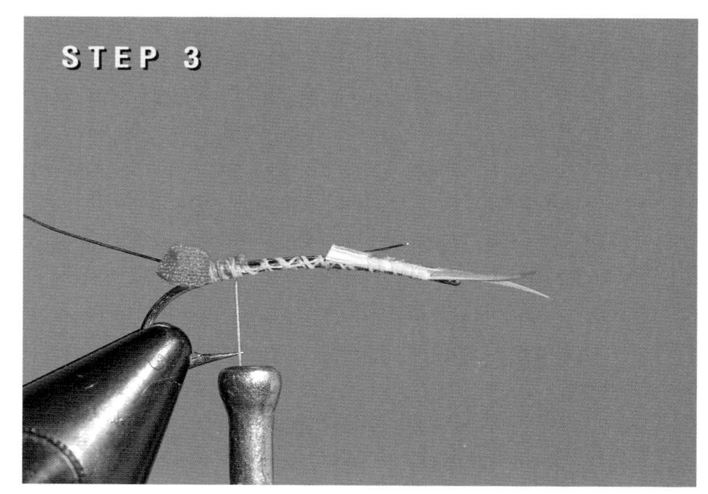

Tie in a small piece of red 2 mm foam. It should extend from the shank above the barb to the end of the bend.

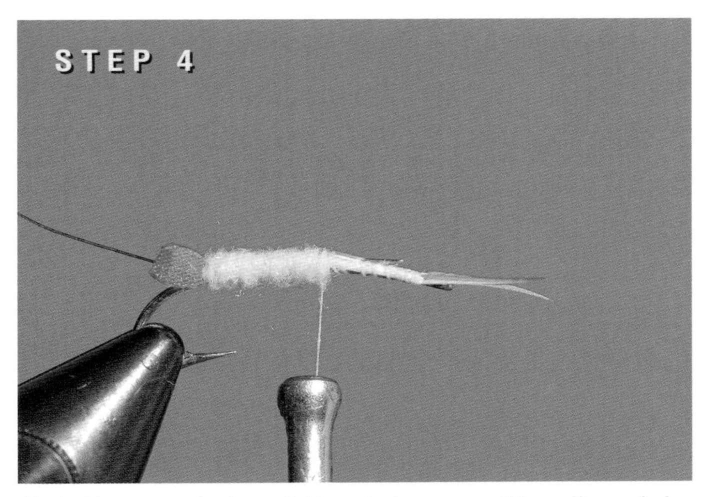

Dub the remainder of the abdomen with yellow dubbing—it should extend just past mid-shank.

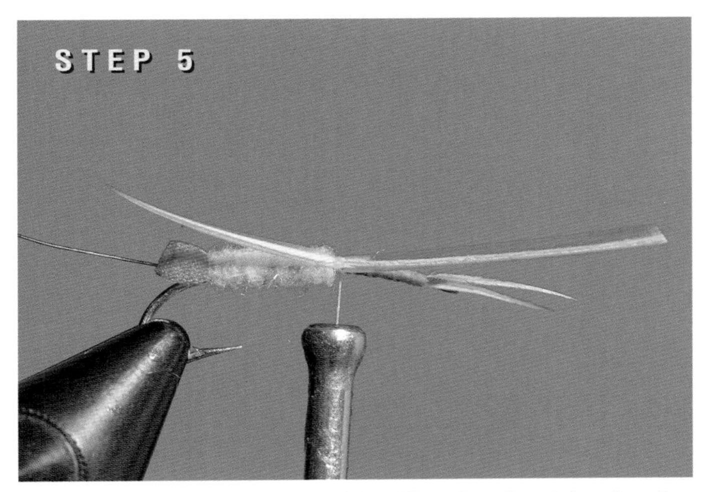

Tie in a biot on the near side. The tip should extend a third of a shank length past the hook bend.

Repeat step 5 on the far side of body. Make sure the tips match, and then finish securing the biots.

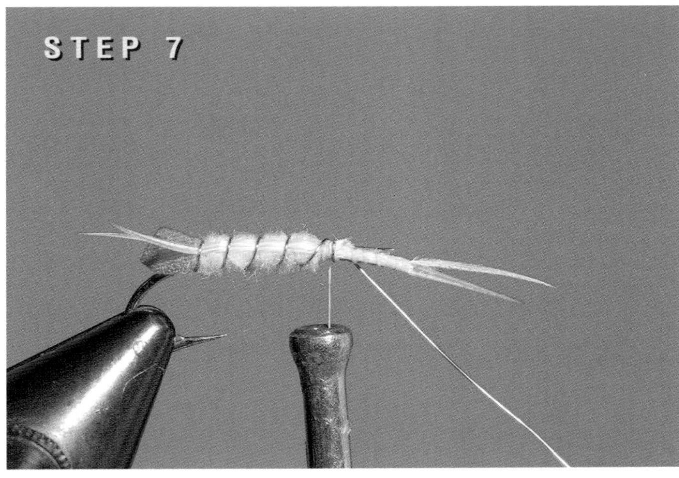

Make a wrap around the rear of the body with the copper wire. After this, hold the near biot against the body and lash it in place against the body. Hold the far biot against the body and secure it with the wire. Continue ribbing the biot/body combo with the wire. Make a few wraps with wire in the thorax area, tie it down, and cut it off.

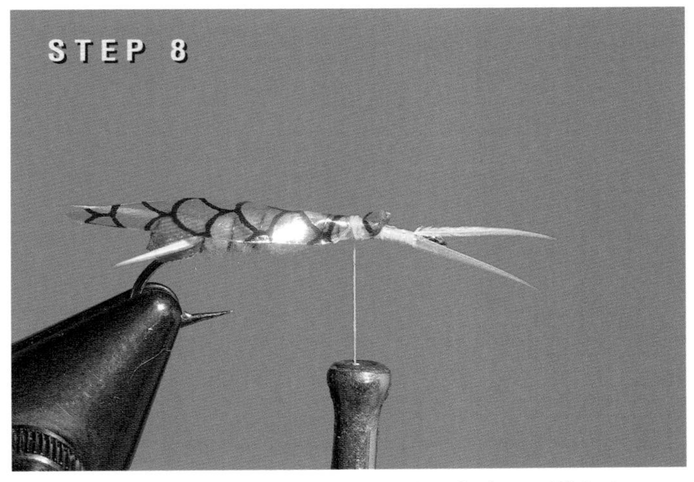

Stick pearl lure tape to a clear plastic bag. This keeps the sticky tape from adhering to the body. Other film wing materials can also be used. Cut out a wing one hook-gap wide and the length of the shank. Make it look like a willow leaf. Secure the wing in the thorax area and cement the wraps.

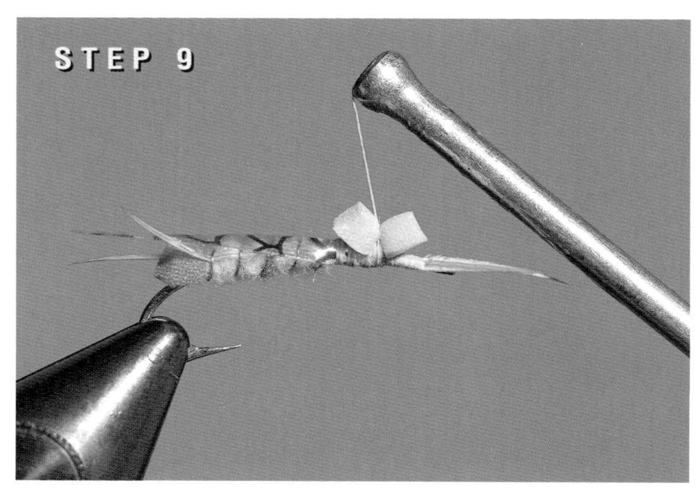

Tie in a wedge-style foam indicator at the middle of the thorax.

Tie in the hackle at the rear of the thorax.

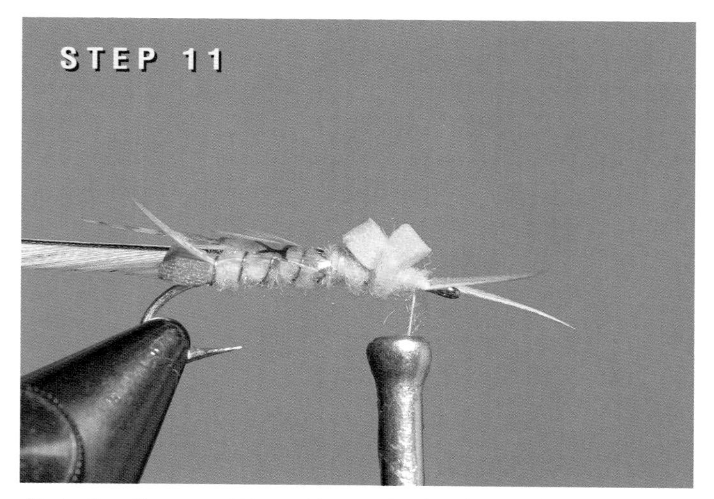

Dub the thorax. Wrap through the foam indicator.

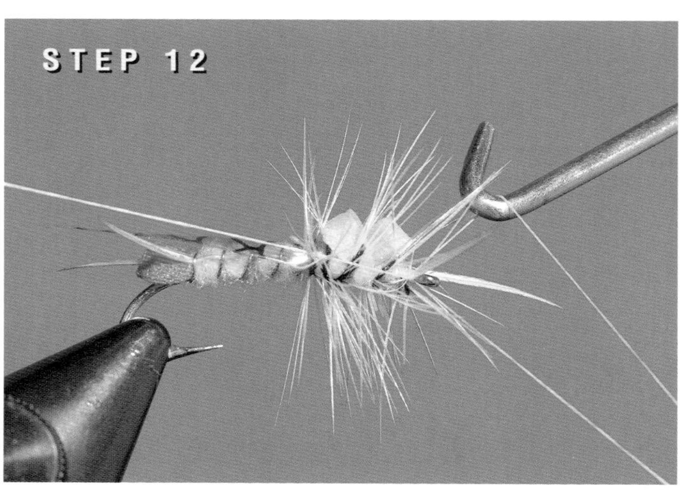

Wrap the hackle through the thorax and tie it off. Whip-finish and cement.

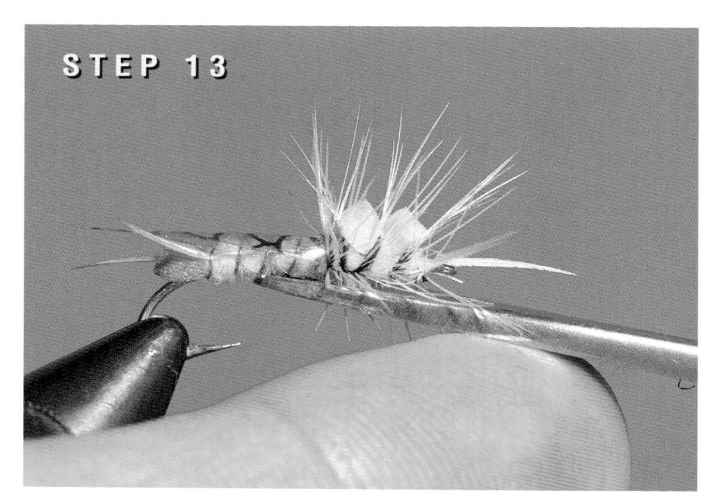

Trim the hackle flush on the belly of the fly. This makes the body of the fly float flush on the water's surface.

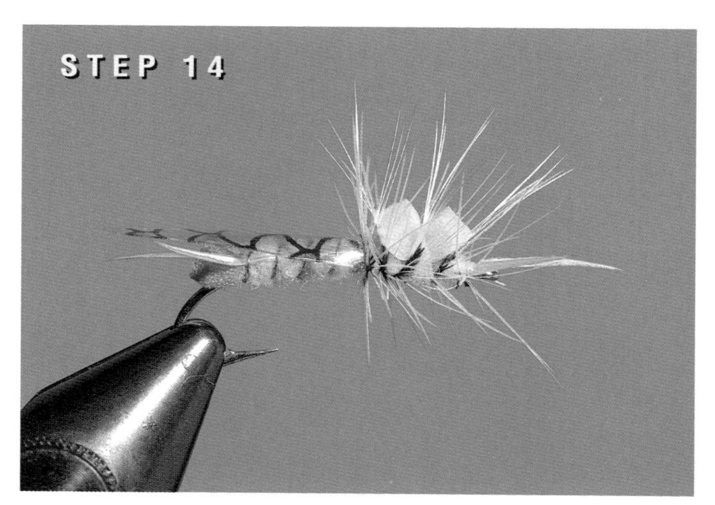

The finished fly.

Spandex Stone

THE SNAKE RIVER IN WYOMING AND IDAHO has robust hatches of large stoneflies. They start with the big golden stones in April, proceed through the salmonflies in July, and continue with brown stones in August and September. The trout feed aggressively on these big bugs, and in many cases the nymphs are more important than adult dries. The large nymphs have a life cycle of as many as four years. They're found in the stream drift throughout the year. However, they are much more significant during hatch periods, when they become more active and are plentiful. An effective stonefly nymph is basic to western angling.

Because I designed this fly to be dead-drifted, I wanted flexible legs that would move with the current. Other fine rubbers can break from casting but Spandex is the strongest of the fine rubbers—it's almost unbreakable.

I wanted a fairly realistic stonefly that didn't require a great deal of time to tie. The idea for this fly came from a feather-back golden stonefly nymph that Pat Berry showed me. Pat worked with me at Jack Dennis Sports, and on an April fishing excursion on the Snake he was having great luck with his Eastern Golden Stone. I liked the look of the fly, but I wanted more motion. Spandex (Super Floss, Flexi Floss, Spanflex) had just come on the fly-tying market. The material looks like floss but is actually rubber. I wondered if it could replace the turkey back and possibly be used for legs.

Because I designed this fly to be dead-drifted, I wanted flexible legs that would move with the current. Other fine rubbers can break from casting, but Spandex is the strongest of the fine rubbers—it's almost unbreakable. In addition, it absorbs water and comes in many attractive colors. To weight the fly, I put two beads on the hook, one at the head and one in the thorax.

I first fished the Spandex Stone on the Snake during the spring pre-runoff season, catching trout and plenty of whitefish. Hey, a tug is a tug! Later that year, I used the new pattern on the South Fork and Henry's Fork with impressive results. I've since used it to fool fish on stonefly waters throughout Montana.

This fly can usually be fished without the extra weight of split-shot. While I'm not adverse to fishing with shot, there are times when working boulder runs and riprap that I want to be in contact with my fly. If you have lead on the leader, you get a hinge in the leader and lose contact with the fly. This results in missed fish and hang-ups. The double-bead weighting allows it to be bounced along structure like a jig. (For some situations, I add lead wire along with beads.) The fly has the right amount of weight if it hurts when it hits you. To fish these conditions, I use a long tippet of 2X or 1X and keep the fly line out of the water. You flip the fly into the run or pocket,

SPANDEX STONE

HOOK:	Dai-Riki 270 or 280 natural-bend, sizes 4 to 10.
THREAD:	Yellow 3/0.
TAIL:	Tan goose biots.
RIB:	Yellow 3/0 thread.
BACK:	Six strands of tan Super Floss (Spandex).
ABDOMEN:	Golden brown dubbing.
WINGCASES:	Remainder of the back Spandex.
THORAX:	Body dubbing and a copper bead.
LEGS:	The tips of the wing cases, three strands on each side.
HEAD:	Copper bead.
ANTENNAE:	Tan goose biots.

let it sink, and then keep slight tension on the fly. You'll feel strikes and the bottom. You can also lift the fly up and down to imitate a dislodged nymph.

This fly and technique have provided hours of urban trout entertainment on the Yellowstone along the city-park dike in Livingston, Montana. This town section has the highest trout population on the Yellowstone—only four blocks from my house. During the high water common to large stonefly hatches, the fish are packed in the soft water created by the riprap. I could walk along and bounce the big nymph through hundreds of pockets and count on fish grabbing my offering. Sweet. People aren't the only creatures that play at the park.

The double-bead weighting allows it to be bounced along structure like a jig. (For some situations, I add lead wire along with beads.) The fly has the right amount of weight if it hurts when it hits you.

I tie this fly in tan or black for fishing the West. I have also tied small olive ones for New Zealand anglers. Midwest anglers to whom I've shown this pattern have adapted it to a *Hexagenia* nymph by using ostrich herl for the abdomen. The Spandex Stone catches fish north and south of the equator.

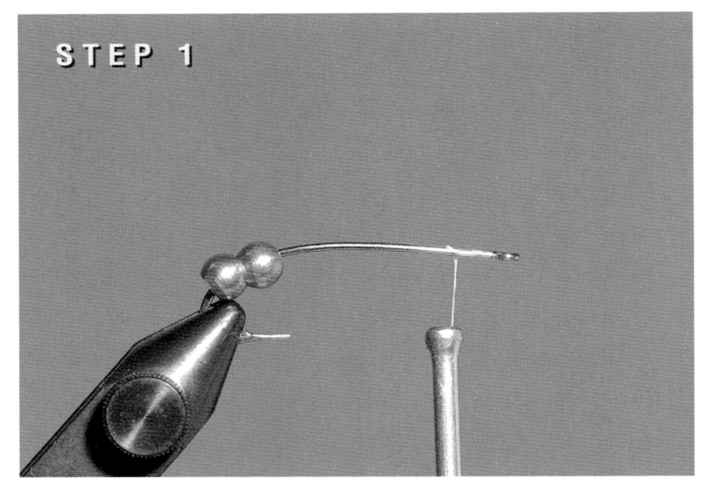

Slide two copper beads on the hook shank. Push the beads back and start your thread behind the hook eye.

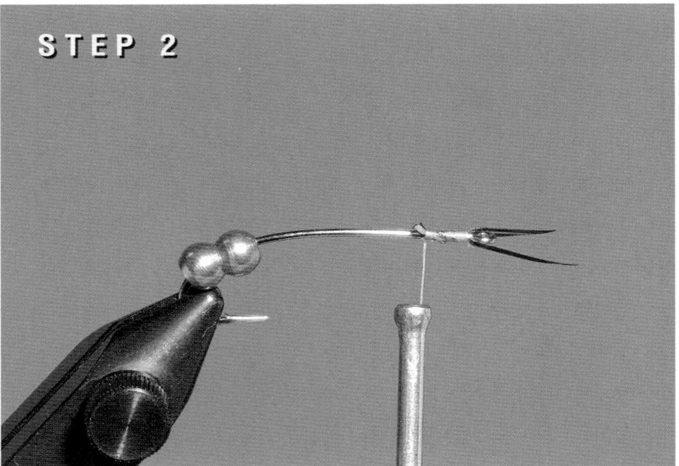

Behind the hook eye, tie on two biots as antennae. Hold them by the butts with the curved sides out and use the hook shank to divide the tips. You want them a quarter of a shank length long. Do a quick whip finish or half hitch and cut your thread.

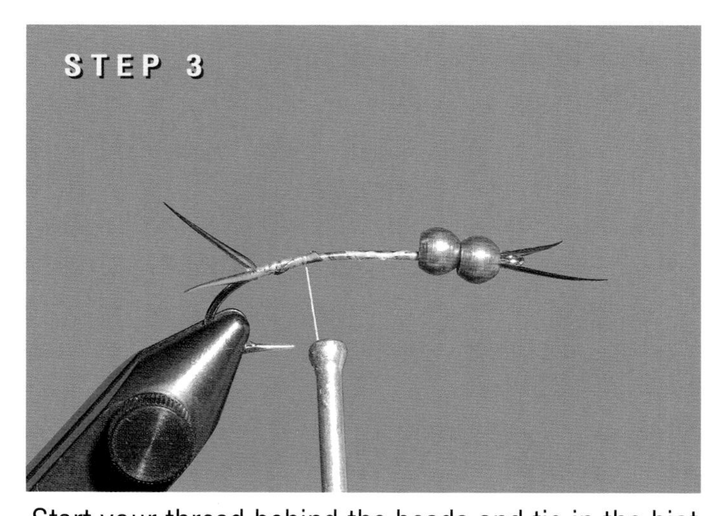

Start your thread behind the beads and tie in the biot tails. Arrange the tips curved sides out in your left hand and slide the butts over the hook shank to divide them. Secure these on the hook shank above the barb.

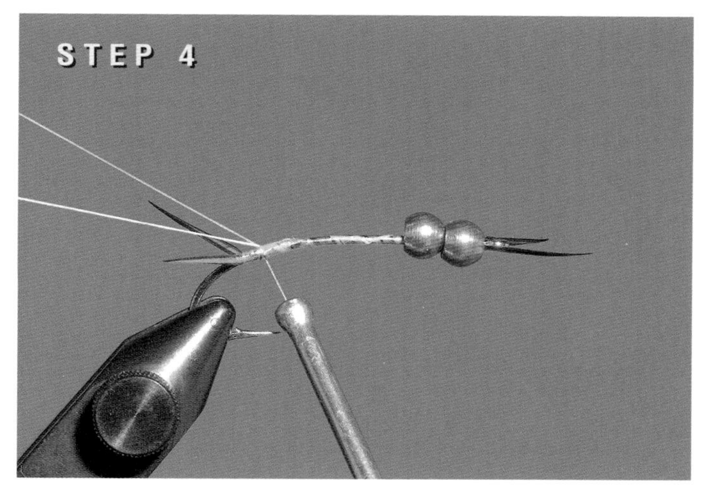

Tie on a double strand of yellow 3/0 thread or make a dubbing loop with the tying thread. This will be the rib. Pull it to the far side of hook shank and stick it in your material clip.

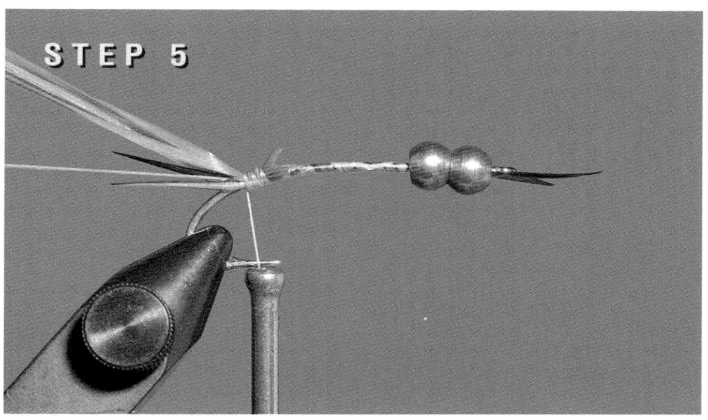

Tie in six strands of Spandex, each about three shank-lengths long. These will be on the top of the hook shank. You can clip them into a material clip if desired.

We'll dub the abdomen in layers because it is difficult to make enough dubbing adhere to the thread at once to create a thick body—this saves time and frustration. Bring your thread up to approximately one third of the shank length from the eye. Apply dubbing to your thread. Wrap this back to the Spandex. Add more dubbing to the thread and wrap it forward.

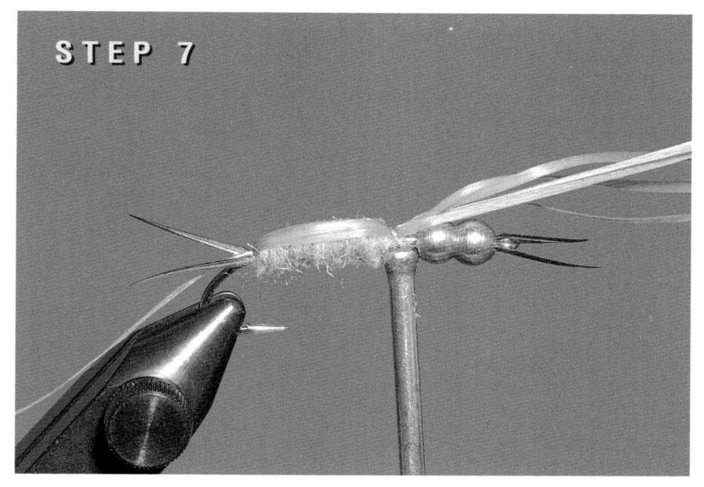

Pull the Spandex over the abdomen and tie it off.

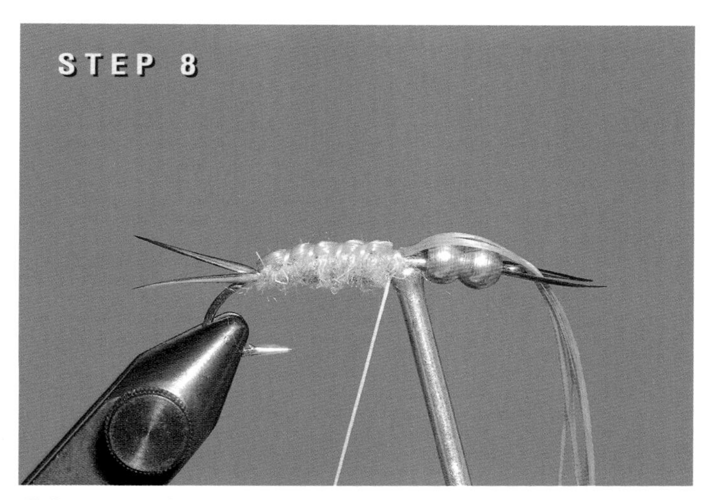

Take your rib thread and rib over the abdomen with tension. Your first wrap should over the dubbing belly and then onto the Spandex back—this keeps the thread from rolling back over to the side. The flexibility of the rubber and the soft dubbing will segment perfectly.

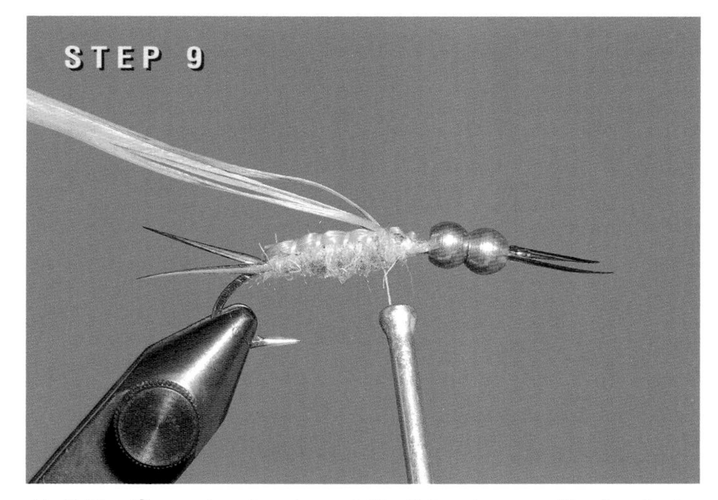

Pull the Spandex back and tie it back over the body to mid-shank. This builds up the thorax.

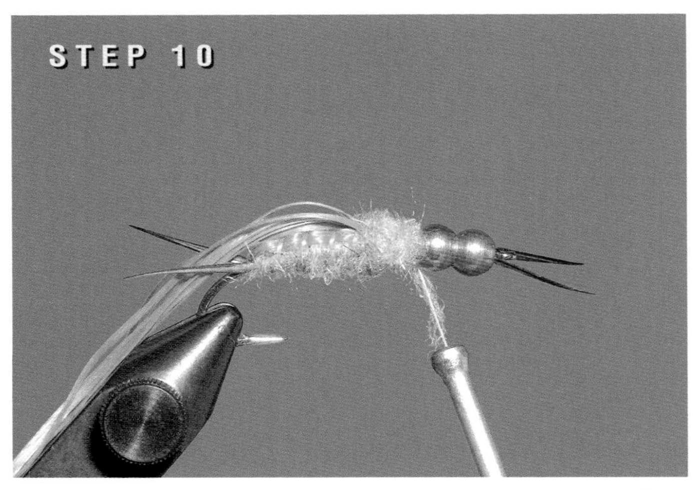

Dub the thorax almost up to the first bead. This should be larger in diameter than the abdomen. Leave a slight space behind the bead.

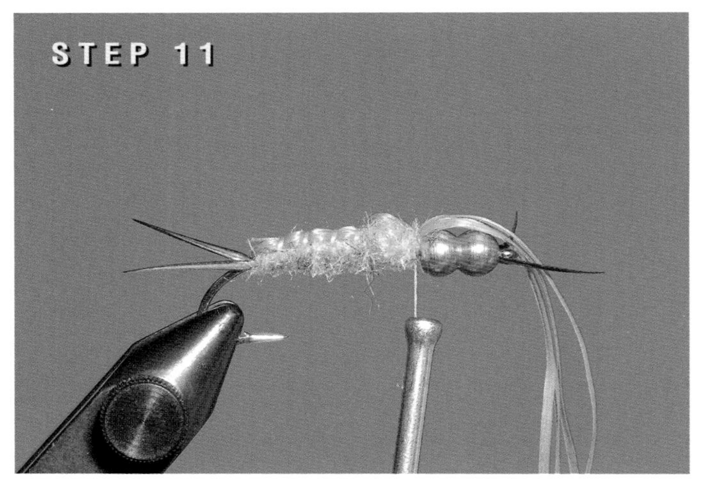

Pull the Spandex over as the first wing case and secure it.

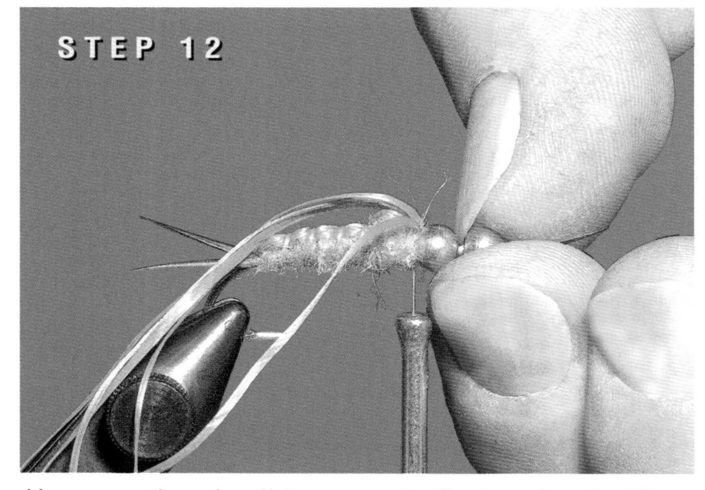

Use your thumbnail to separate the two beads. Then wrap your thread over the top of the bead and around the hook shank a few times.

Pull the Spandex over the bead to form the second wing case and secure it with thread between the two beads. To make sure the thread is against the hook shank, push the material and thread down with your thumbnail.

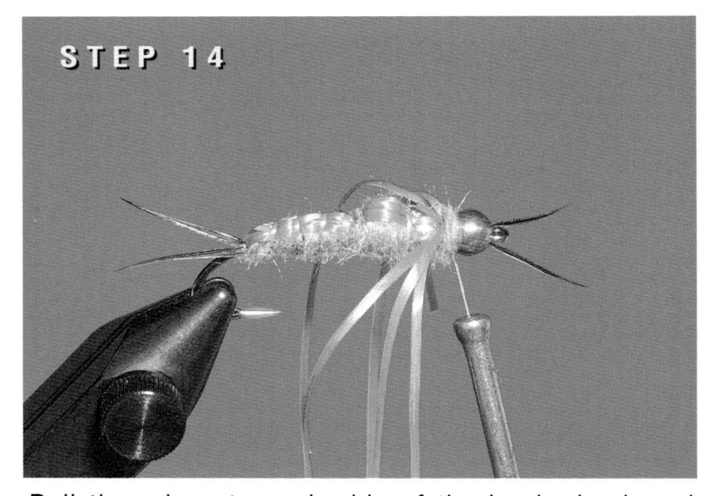

Pull three legs to each side of the hook shank and wrap them in place with your thread. To hold them in position, add a small amount of dubbing to the thread to make a "neck." (The friction of the dubbing makes it easier to keep the legs where you pulled them.)

Whip-finish behind the bead. Make sure the thread is against the hook shank by pushing the thread down with your thumbnail and then pulling the whip finish tight. Trim the legs to the length of the shank.

The finished fly.

CHAPTER 5

MIDGES

MIDGES ARE THE ONLY MAJOR TROUT FOOD that hatches all year long. What they lack in size they make up for in numbers and frequency. Midges provide the first and last dry-fly fishing of the year. Their diversity of habitat is amazing—they thrive in scum ponds as well as in gigantic rivers.

Midges are common aquatic insects. On many waters they may be the most numerous insects. Anglers generally associate this bug with tailwaters, but the tiny chironomids are found in most water types. Large western rivers such as the Snake, Yellowstone, Madison, Gallatin, and lower Henry's Fork have outstanding fall, late-winter, and spring hatches. Although these waters have a freestone look and quality to them, heavy midge hatches typically bring out large quantities of rising fish; they can rival many tailwaters and spring creeks.

Midge X

On big-hatch days, the fish feed more aggressively than their spring-creek cousins. Concentrations of rising fish are a welcome sight after a long winter of frozen fingers and nymph fishing. These warming, promising days offer opportunities for some of the most consistent match-the-hatch fishing of the year.

Midges and winter trout prefer moderate currents. You won't find fish feeding out in the middle of the river. For the trout, slower currents demand less expenditure of energy than faster summer lies. And midge activity seems to be heavier in these flows. Another factor is the accumulation of insects pushed into slack water by wind and water. When nature puts out a meal, the trout will come. Inside corners, back eddies, slower troughs, and tailouts hold the most insects and fish. Some of the trout move into surprisingly shallow water to take advantage of this food source, with the best ones adjacent to the comfort of deeper water. Riseforms can be exceptionally subtle. It takes a watchful eye to spot them. Back eddies covered in foam hold numerous fish. As the foam moves with the current, the fish move with it to follow the collected food—and keep a roof over their heads. These fish can be tough. Many times they are the largest trout.

Concentrations of rising fish are a welcome sight after a long winter of frozen fingers and nymph fishing. These warming, promising days offer opportunities for some of the most consistent match-the-hatch fishing of the year.

I like to use an 81/2- to 9-foot 4- or 5-weight rod for midge fishing. The length helps with mending. Spring and fall winds can be a factor. On the Yellowstone—where I once had two size 12 bead heads blown out of my hand—I sometimes use my 6-weight. I favor a medium-action rod such as a Scott PowerPly. Your rod should have adequate power to cast into the wind, with a tip sensitive enough to protect light tippets.

Nine- to 10-foot leaders tapered to 4X or 5X tippets suffice for much of the big-river fishing. I use three-foot tippets to help with the drift. I like soft materials such as Dai-Riki Dynamic. If you work a pod of fish for a while, you might need 6X. Low-angle winter light can cause a high level of surface glare. As you will see throughout this book, many of my floating flies have features than help with visibility. You will get a better drift if you know where your fly is.

Although one can't pick the weather, the best fishing and hatch days are relatively warm and overcast. Light precipitation (usually snow) can come down, but it's likely to bother the angler more than the trout. Afternoon fishing is usually the best as this is the warmer part of the day.

Emerging midges frequently mingle with other insects. *Baetis* and small black stoneflies frequent the same waters on late-winter and early spring days. Later on, caddisflies might be present. As the weather warms, these other hatches become more important.

This chapter will cover some of flies that have proved effective during winter and spring midge hatches. Over the years, these flies have been the keys to some memorable days. They have produced consistent results on many different waters.

Midge X

Sometimes an idea for a fly is so obvious that we overlook it. Many fertile ideas are lurking at our tying benches. Sometimes we just need a little push to discover them. This was the case with the Midge X. I've fished Madam X-style patterns for years. With a modification in size and color, a plethora of insects can be imitated. The difference between this midge and its predecessors is that the "legs" imitate bodies instead of appendages. This little sister of the original could be called a Miss X, since she is too small to be a Madam.

This pattern is an imitation of a midge cluster. During heavy hatches, clusters of spent or crippled

MIDGE X

HOOK: Dai Riki 125, sizes 14 to 18.

THREAD: Black Gudebrod 8/0 or 10/0.

BODIES: Black, brown, or olive Angler's Choice Bodeez 'N' Legz or Hedron Perfect Rubber.

THORAXES: Sparse dubbing matching the natural insect's body color around the post and the base of the legs.

POST: White, black, or fluorescent-pink Antron or poly yarn to match light conditions.

HACKLE: Grizzly tied parachute style, two gap-widths in length.

Clusters of adults floated down; the back eddies were becoming covered with them. This was a perfect chance to try my new fly. I tied one on and immediately caught some healthy rainbows out of a slick.

adults normally pile up in soft currents and back eddies. Many square feet of foam lines and eddies are littered with the bodies. On lakes, the wind and waves will stack them up on the lee shore. While one bug might be a snack, a mouthful of them is a meal, and injured or dead insects won't run away. This is the all-you-can-eat snack-food buffet.

These dense, year-round hatches are amazing. What they lack in size they make up in biomass, although some stillwater species don't fit the connotation of "midge" and are imitated with hook sizes up to 12. When I lived near the Yellowstone River, the sides of my house were a good indicator of what was hatching on the water. Mayflies and caddisflies made short annual visits to the neighborhood, but midges are there 12 months of the year. This is true of most western waters. Even on famous spring creeks and tailwaters, chironomids cover the calendar year.

The Midge X has roots in other common patterns as well. The all-encompassing Parachute Adams is a reliable midge imitation with the added bonus of visibility to the angler. Hold this fly up to the light. Take a look at it from the bottom and you will understand why a trout might take it for a midge. The parachute's visibility helps the angler track the drift of his fly to assure drag-free presentation. It also lets you know that the fish ate your fly and not a natural. This is important: Mistakenly setting the hook when a natural is sipped next to your imitation is likely to spook the trout and put them down for a while.

When I came up with this fly, I was working on improving the appearance of double-spinner patterns commonly fished during Trico hatches. By tying two spinners on a single hook shank, you can fish a larger fly. This has a number of benefits. A larger fly is easier to see. A larger hook helps hook more fish—it's less prone to straightening out or pulling out. And the drifts of larger artificials are less affected by tippet size.

While playing with the double-spinner patterns, I tried some double-extended bodies. This can be fairly difficult on small flies, and only a few materials are suitable. Larva Lace was one option. Tying in a double-extended body of Larva Lace reminded me of the numerous X-legs flies that have come out of my vise. Rubber came to mind. The fly would be missing the tails found on mayflies, but it might make a great midge. Perfect Rubber or Bodeez 'N' Legs could be used to make mottled, translucent bodies.

With some time on the water, my mind was in the mood to imitate the Yellowstone's heavy March midge hatches. I tied up some prototypes and on a cool March morning I cruised to one of my favorite in-town pools to give them a try. Early fishing required sunken midge pupae with an indicator. As the temperature warmed and trout backs became visible, I switched to my version of a Parachute Midge Emerger. With further warming, the hatch escalated. Clusters of adults floated down; the back eddies were becoming covered with them. This was a perfect chance to try my new fly. I tied one on and immediately caught some healthy rainbows out of a slick. The ultimate test of a fishing fly is a trout's approval—I apparently had it. My new creation caught fish in pools, tailouts, back eddies and riffles. Three hours later it was still gulped eagerly by feeding fish.

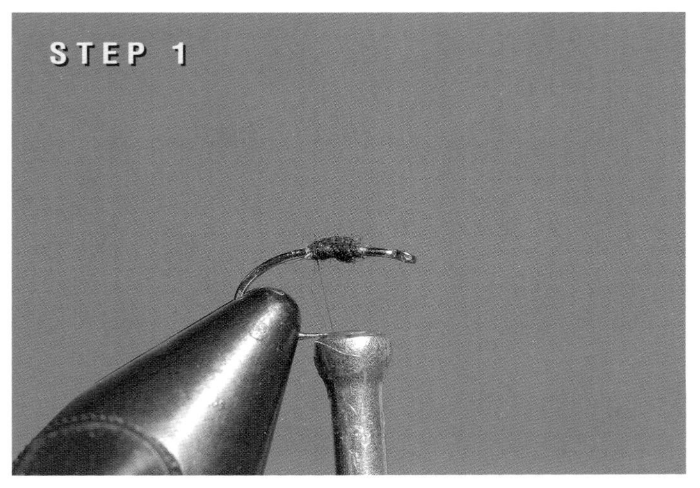

Super-glue the middle of the hook shank and make a thread base on the middle quarter of the shank. Add a very small amount of dubbing to the middle of the shank as a base.

Take a strand of Antron and fold it around the thread. With your thread, pull the center of the Antron down onto the hook shank and secure it.

Post the Antron wing. Make a firm post with thread and then make figure-eight wraps around the base of the post and hook shank.

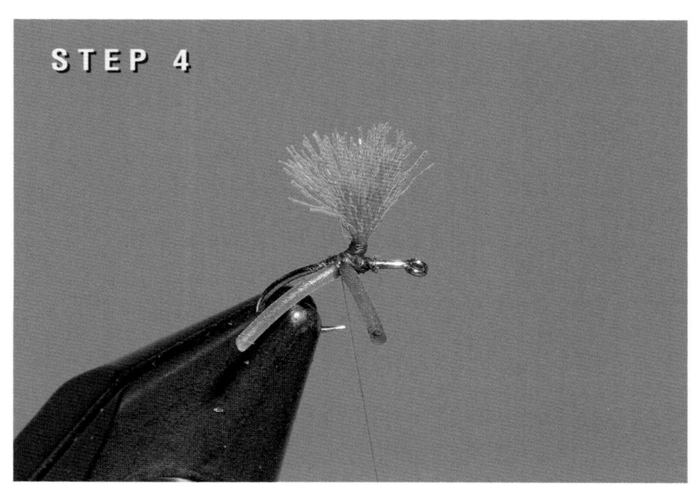

Tie in a rubber leg X-style on the near side of the hook just behind the post—this will create two legs.

Repeat step 4 on the far side and then trim all four legs to one shank length each.

Tie in a grizzly hackle and lightly dub around the post.

Wrap the hackle and tie it off.

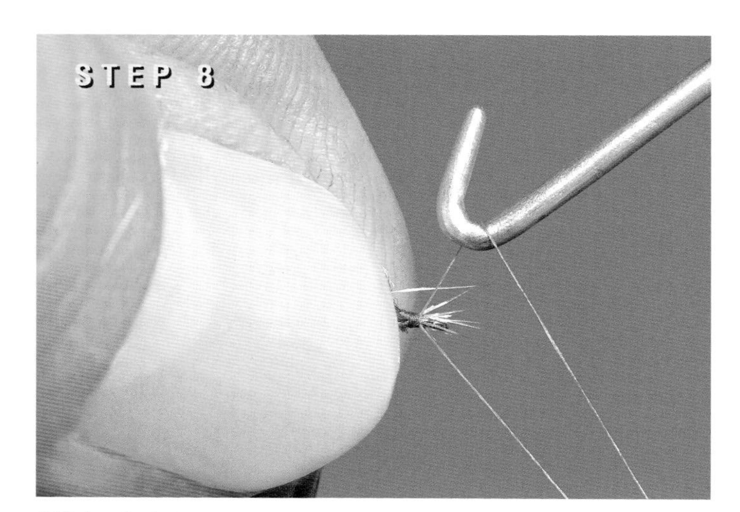

Whip-finish and cement.

The finished fly.

Parachute Midge Emerger

THE PARACHUTE MIDGE EMERGER IS A COMPILATION of several different patterns. It's an almost "non-refusal" fly when trout are rising to emerging midge pupae. This is my fly of choice when I see midging fish whose backs are breaking the surface, but whose snouts aren't. These fish are eating pupae just under the surface and will ignore standard dry flies.

Here's what's going on: The pupae frequently get caught in the surface film in a horizontal position. Depending on conditions, the pupae can drift a distance before escaping the surface tension. Trout key in on such easy meals.

The buoyant materials at the head of the fly make that portion float, while the body is subsurface—this is what the natural midge pupa does.

When I came up with this fly, I borrowed ideas from the English "buzzer" patterns, Quigley Cripples, and my own Ultra Zug nymph. The cripple patterns are part dry fly and part nymph. The buoyant materials at the head of the fly makes that portion float, while the body is subsurface—this is what the natural midge pupa does. The peacock and pearl Ultra Zug had been my top lake fly during midge hatches, so I decided to modify it to a suspended pupa for winter midge hatches.

Some of my early trials with the fly were on the Snake downstream of Astoria Hot Springs. This section is always a few degrees warmer than the rest of the river, harboring winter trout and producing more winter hatches. Depth and moderate currents also add to the allure. When late-afternoon hatches come off, fish are lined up along the bank and behind large rocks. With a Parachute Emerger and a good drift over a rising fish, you will usually get a strike. It definitely works better than a surface pattern. I've had good results with it on the Yellowstone, Madison, and Green rivers, and on the Livingston spring creeks. I tie the fly with a white or orange indicator. I also tie the body with olive or claret dubbing.

The Parachute Midge Emerger makes an effective strike indicator for a sunken midge pupae. A loop knot (my favorite is the nonslip mono loop) will ensure that the fly lands correctly each time. Grease the hackle and wing so that the body hangs vertically below the surface.

PARACHUTE MIDGE EMERGER

HOOK:	Dai-Riki 305 standard dry fly, sizes 16 to 22.
THREAD:	Black 10/0.
INDICATOR:	White or orange synthetic fibers or foam.
TAG:	One or two strands of pearl Krystal Flash cut short.
RIB:	Pearl Krystal Flash.
BODY:	Scintilla No. 46 Peacockle dubbing.
HACKLE:	A few wraps of grizzly; the fibers should be one gap-width long.

Cement hook shank and start the thread. Tie on the Antron indicator over the eye of the hook; you want it as long as the hook shank. Wrap thread in front of the indicator to slightly lift it—this will make it easier to attach the tippet when fishing.

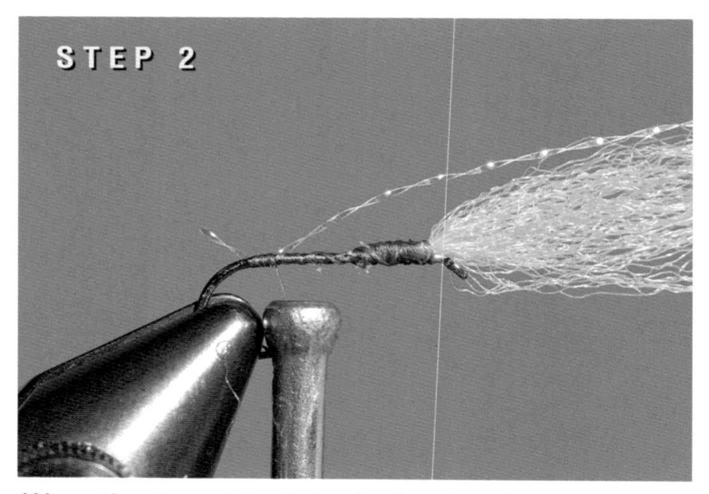

Wrap the thread back to the bend and tie in a short tail of Krystal Flash. Trim all but one of the butt strands—this will be the rib.

Dub a sparse body on three quarters of the hook shank. On small flies, a few dubbing fibers are all you need.

Rib the body with Krystal Flash and tie it off

Tie in a grizzly hackle and make two or three wraps. Tie it off. If extra flotation is needed, use more hackle wraps or a larger hackle.

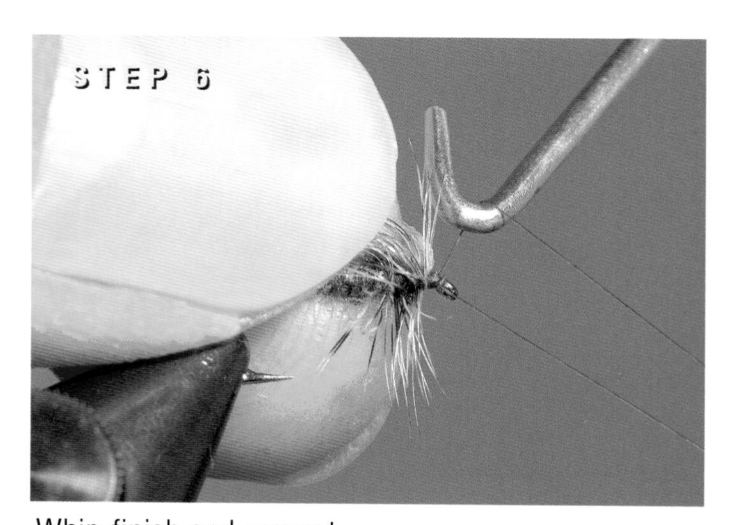

Whip-finish and cement.

The finished fly in the position it will adopt in the water.

CHAPTER 6

VERSATILE EMERGERS AND CRIPPLES

FOR TROUT TO SURVIVE, THEY NEED TO BE EFFICIENT FEEDERS—their daily challenge is to get more calories from their prey than they exert in capturing it. The best food sources are easy to capture, abundant, and predictable. It makes sense for fish to seek out these foods and feed aggressively when they find them. Emerging and crippled aquatic insects match this optimum feeding scenario and are essential to trout survival. The corresponding patterns are important when casting to selective trout because they imitate these vulnerable insects.

It is easier to understand the feeding behavior of trout during a hatch if we strip it down to the basics.

Everything Emerger

A hatch is a propagation migration not unlike other animal movements. The bugs are throwing caution to the wind in an effort to create another generation. As nature dictates, the survival of the species is more important than the survival of the individual. Emergence is a time of transition and vulnerability. At times during this event, insects won't have a full complement of either nymph or adult escape mechanisms or camouflage at their disposal. Evolution is at play here. The weak are eliminated; predators eat them. As with migrations of mammals or fish, the paths of emerging insects are fairly predictable: Rather than hunt for their food, the trout can sit and wait for it to come to them. This happens time and time again in nature. While a 16-inch brown waiting for a delicate little mayfly may seem less bloody than wolves waiting for moving caribou, both are basically the same thing—a Discovery Channel special about predators and prey.

If you were a trout, would you go for a pale morning dun wriggling on the surface, stuck in its nymphal shuck, or a fully emerged dun ready to fly off?

Predators go after weak prey before they chase healthy ones. The weak are easier to catch. And crippled insects are just weak or injured prey. If you were a trout, would you go for a pale morning dun wriggling on the surface, stuck in its nymphal shuck, or a fully emerged dun ready to fly off? Certain characteristics enable predators to pick out and attack injured prey in preference to surrounding specimens. A lion may look for a limping wildebeest, while a trout might look for the profile of a insect struggling in a nymphal shuck. Both signify an easy meal—this is as much efficiency as selectivity. The emergers are vulnerable because they are in an area where fish are feeding and the cripples are particularly vulnerable because they are immobile in the presence of predators

The good news about cripples is that although we fish many different hatches, most of them can be covered with a few patterns. In many cases, the difference between an emerger and a cripple is the time spent in transition between nymph and adult. Even though caddisflies, stoneflies, mayflies, and midges have distinctive shapes as larvae and adults, in the emerging and crippled forms their appearances are similar. If you look at a fly catalog, you'll notice many of the emerger patterns are similar regardless of insect family. Prominent features in most natural cripples and surface-area emergers are a nymphal shuck attached to a segmented body with struggling legs and an emerging wing. My Everything Emerger covers those key features. When tied in various sizes and colors, the pattern covers a good a variety of hatches.

A soft-hackle emerger is another very basic fly that covers many different insects well enough for most fishing situations. The Ultra Zug series, Foam-Back Sparkle Dun, and the Parachute Midge Emerger covered in other sections of this book round out my emergers. Although these flies aren't the cure-all during all hatches,they have consistently produced over tough fish. I can fish them confidently during hatches around the world.

Everything Emerger

The Everything Emerger is my favorite all-purpose emerger. This fly in a few colors and sizes covers a myriad of hatches. It is favored by trout internationally. I came up with this pattern while fishing the confusing multiple hatches on the Henry's Fork—it was created on my dashboard in the Last Chance parking lot.

Many streams have selective fish, but typically have only one hatch going on at a time. On this fabled water, however, different hatches at the same time seem to be the norm. Is that fish taking a PMD dun, a speckled sedge, or a yellow Sally? Sometimes the exact food item is easy to decipher; at other times, you're left shaking your head.

EVERYTHING EMERGER

HOOK:	Dai Riki 320 standard dry-fly hook, sizes 12 to 20.
THREAD:	Rust brown 8/0.
SHUCK:	Brown Antron or Z-Lon.
RIB:	Doubled rust-brown tying thread.
BODY:	Tan dubbing.
WING:	Dark elk or deer hair.
LEGS:	Butts of the wing.
THORAX:	Body dubbing wrapped through the legs.

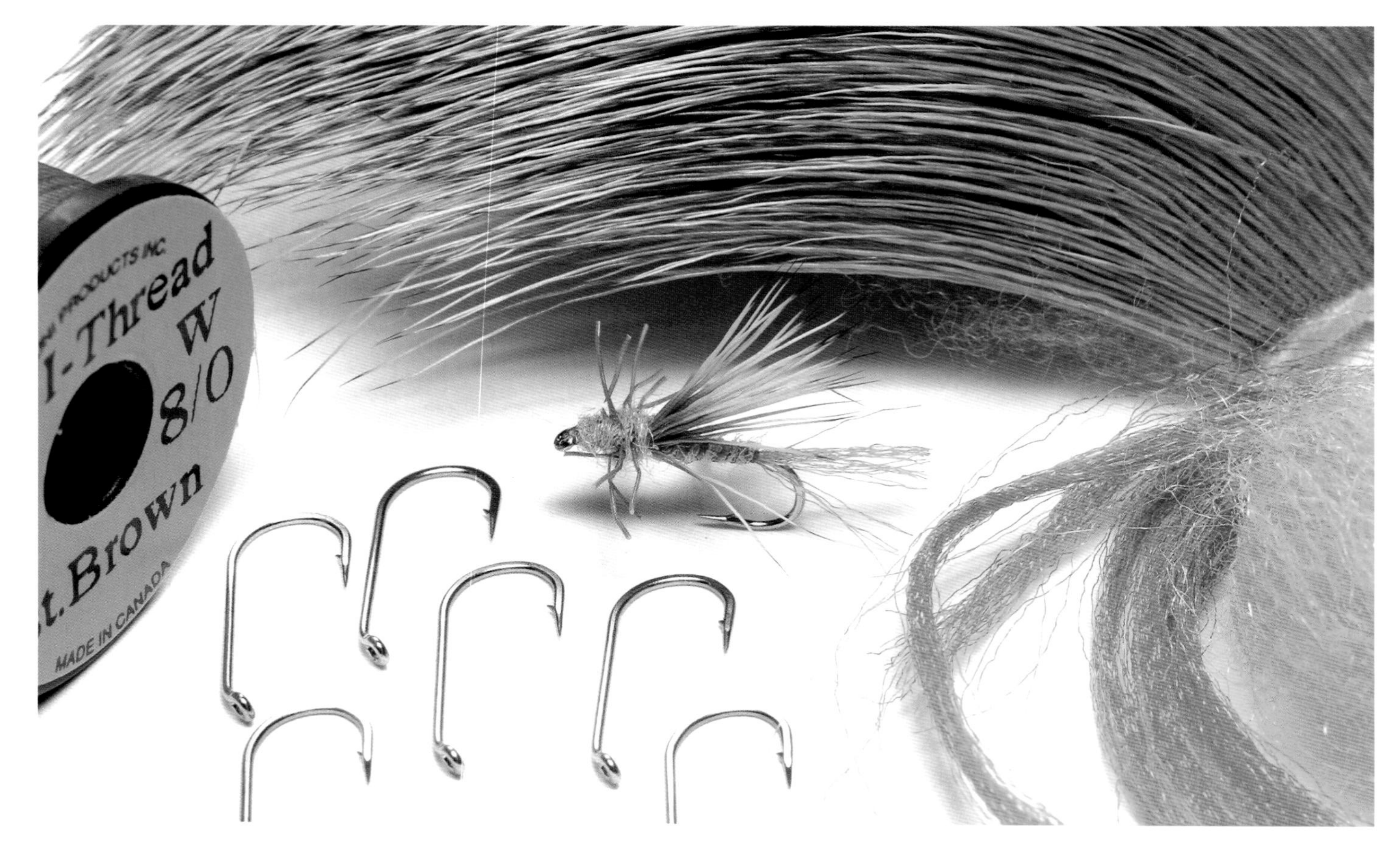

Most aquatic cripples have a similar profile. A crippled insect has a nymphal shuck, a segmented body, a wing in various stages of emergence and discombobulated legs—all which scream, "Oh *shit*, I'm in trouble!" to a trout.

My favorite fly-fishing books—*Selective Trout* and *Fly Fishing Strategies*, by Doug Swisher and Carl Richards, and *Whitlock's Guide to Aquatic Foods*, by Dave Whitlock—support my own observations. Most aquatic cripples have a similar profile. A crippled insect has a nymphal shuck, a segmented body, a wing in various stages of emergence, and discombobulated legs—all which scream, "Oh *shit*, I'm in trouble!" to a trout.

Would a generic emerger work for different insects? I was willing to try. I took a Mathews X Caddis and added a few extras. I used thread to rib the body and used the butts of the wing to make disarrayed legs. These additions, along with the original X Caddis template, seemed to cover the most important feeding triggers for trout. To change the wing profile for different insects, I pulled from fishing experience on the South Fork.

On the South Fork, pale morning duns and yellow Sally stones hatch at the same time. We were using a Harrop Hair-Wing Dun for the PMDs and found that if we smashed down the wing, the fly would work for a yellow Sally. They were both the same color and had forked tails. I transferred this modification idea to the emerger. If you fluff up the wing you have a crippled mayfly—push the wing down and you have a crippled caddis, stonefly, or midge.

I tied some of the flies and was ready to try them. I'd like to tell you I went to down the river and knocked them dead, but that doesn't happen on this technical water. I can report that the new Everything Emerger kept pace with more specific emergers.

I've since added olive, gray, and peacock versions to my original tan fly. I usually use rust thread for the rib since this color seems common on aquatic insects, but I also use olive and dark gray thread to segment the body. Technically, the shuck color should match the color of the nymph, but I find that simply having the shuck makes more difference than choosing the exact color.

My most exotic adventures with the Everything Emerger came during two different trips to France. My wife is a Francophile and spent some time in high school and college there. I have a bad habit of taking fly rods everywhere; on a bicycle tour of France I took a four-piece 4-weight and a 7-weight. Public trout fishing is at a premium in Europe, and coarse fish are the quarry of the common man. With catch-and-decease being the norm, the fish get pretty smart.

We were camping at farm campground in the Loire Valley. It had a stream running through it. I noticed some fish rising. As I sneaked up on them, I discovered they were chubs feeding on caddisflies. At home, I might not go out of my way to catch a chub, but I was in a foreign land. And the fish were rising. I strung up my 4-weight and tied on an Elk Hair Caddis. I figured the chubs would be easy, but all I got was refusals. I dug in my box and I tied on a tan Everything Emerger. I made a few casts and caught my first French fish. I had fooled the wily *Chevesne*. On my next trip, through a friend of a friend of a friend, I was able to fish for trout on the Risle, Charles Ritz's home water. The Everything Emerger came through again. During a spring afternoon caddisfly hatch, I caught eight native brown trout, or *truite fario* as he is known at home.

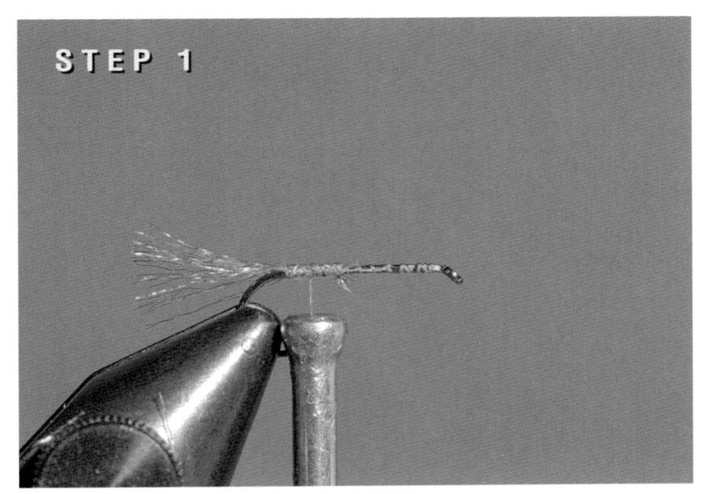

Put a drop of cement on the hook shank and start the thread. Tie in the shuck at the back of the hook. It should be about as long as the shank.

Make a dubbing loop with the tying thread and leave it at the back of hook. This will be the rib.

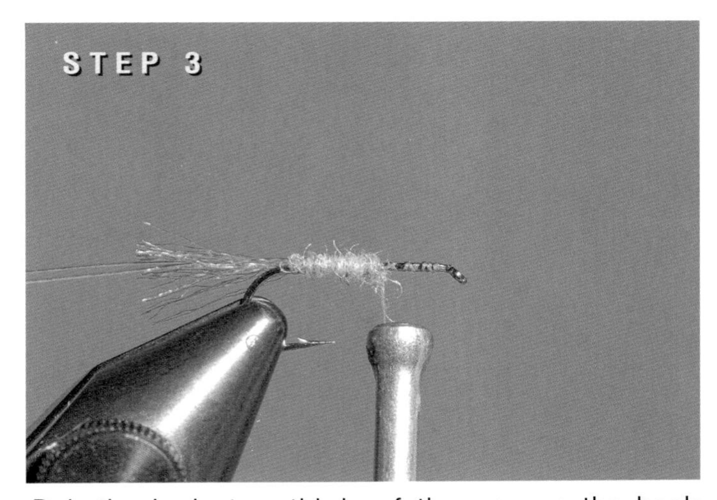

Dub the body two thirds of the way up the hook shank. You will need the front third of the hook for the wings and legs

Twist the doubled thread together, rib the body, and tie off the rib.

Tie in the wing so that the tips extend to the bend of the hook.

Cut out the center part of the hair butts, so that just a few fibers remain on each side of the fly. Cut these so they are about as long as the gap of the hook.

Dub through the wing butts to separate the legs. Figure-eight around the butts and then make a wrap through the middle of the hair fibers.

Whip-finish and cement.

Gently pinch the hair-butt legs. This will cause them to crimp and form jointed legs.

The finished fly.

Soft-Hackle Emergers

A PARTRIDGE AND PHEASANT SOFT-HACKLE was responsible for the best day that I've ever had on the Henry's Fork—or should I say my best two hours of fishing?

On a mid-June day, I was on my way to Last Chance from Livingston. While driving along the Madison River, I noticed that it had cleared from runoff brown to green. The Madison was clear enough to fish. Nobody was there. I couldn't pass up this opportunity. I pulled off at Three Dollar Bridge and had a blast with Double Bunnies. Finally leaving the Madison about 7 p.m., I arrived at Last Chance hungry and tired.

They have a nice subtle action, and their simple shape emulates many aquatic emergers, ovipositing adults, and cripples. They don't look exactly like anything, but they look close enough to many things. In fact, their generic shape may be their best attribute.

I pulled into the A Bar for my usual Texas Burger and a beer. While I enjoyed sustenance, I saw some random rises—one here and one there. It appeared to be a caddisfly situation. Remarkably, no one was on the water. *What the hell*, I thought, and got ready to fish. Wading in, I noticed a couple of dark caddisflies in the air. There was a fish working above the log jam. I caught the small rainbow on a Foam-Wing Caddis, but several larger fish were rising occasionally in the run below. I looked in my fly box and found a couple of size 14 Partridge and Caddis soft-hackles. I tied one on and moved into position. After swinging the fly down the run a few times, I had a solid hit and landed a nice rainbow. This exciting action continued for an hour and half. By the time it was finished I had connected with about 15 fish. Not all were big, but a couple of them were in the 18-inch range, and a number were solid 13- to 16-inch trout. In a couple of hours, I had duplicated a week's worth of catching. As I went back to A Bar to celebrate, the Partridge and Pheasant was probably celebrating its tricentennial.

Soft-hackle wet flies are an ancient but very effective type of fly. The style is one of my favorites for imitating emerging insects. The first flies that were fished were probably soft-hackles. For some reason, fish haven't become wise to them over the years. Thanks to books by Sylvester Nemes and his matching of soft-hackle patterns to natural insects, the flies have regained a modern popularity.

They have a nice subtle action, and their simple shape emulates many aquatic emergers, ovipositing adults, and cripples. They don't look exactly like anything, but they look close enough to many things. In fact, their generic shape may be their best attribute. I also think that the intrinsic sparseness of these flies doesn't spook heavily fished trout. I suspect that at times, when we think trout are taking a soft-hackle for a specific insect, the fish may be eating them as another life form. I like to think I'm in the know, but

OLIVE & GUINEA SOFT HACKLE

HOOK: Dai-Riki 320, sizes 14 to 18.
THREAD: Olive 8/0.
HACKLE: Guinea fowl.
RIB: Brown 6/0 thread.
BODY: Fine olive dubbing.

I also know not to look the proverbial gift horse in the mouth! If it works, go with it.

Soft-hackles can be fished in a number of ways—and you can try different techniques without changing flies. Dead-drifting is an overlooked method. When dressed with floatant, soft-hackles can be used in the surface film as cripples or spent spinners. Without floatant, they sink just below the surface and may be taken as drowned terrestrials or aquatic insects, or as nymphs moving to the surface prior to emergence. Recently, a few sunk-spinner patterns have appeared in the popular fly-fishing literature; in reality these are just dressed-up soft-hackles.

A soft-hackle on the swing is the only technique I've found for consistently catching fish rising randomly in tailouts.

The old wet-fly swing is a deadly method. Dead-drifting flies has become so ingrained in the tactical approach of the modern angler that the ancient wet-fly swing is more often than not ignored. Yet it effectively simulates the movement of some important insects. With one of the most prominent western mayflies, *Baetis*, underwater ovipositing is common: Females dive underwater to lay their eggs. This is also common behavior with a number of prevalent western caddis. A soft-hackle on a controlled swing works as well as anything in these situations. Also, a soft-hackle on the swing is the only technique I've found for consistently catching fish rising randomly in tailouts. Mend your line just enough so that fly swings slightly faster than the current. This takes a little practice but is a deadly technique.

I like to use soft-hackle flies in flat water. They are especially useful for exploring back eddies. Back eddies on our western rivers hold many fish, but their multiple currents and fluctuating speeds make it difficult to present a good drift. A dry fly dragging risks putting off the fish, but a soft-hackle gently moving suggests a struggling pupa. This style of fly makes the best of a tough situation. Use a visible dry fly as an indicator for the soft-hackle if nededTraditionally, most soft-hackles have been tied with upland bird plumage. Hungarian partridge is the most popular material. However, there is a scarcity of small hackles on the skins. I like to fish many of my flies in sizes 14 and smaller. Even if you find a Hun skin with a range of smaller feathers, it will have a slim handful of them and it will cost as much as a genetic dry-fly cape. Other gamebird feathers have thick stems, which don't wrap well. Genetic hen hackle comes in small sizes, but through breeding for the perfect rooster dry-fly hackle, many hen hackles have lost their web. I had a ton of ruffed grouse, pheasant, and guinea fowl feathers in my collection and of these had colors and patterns that would make interesting flies—I just needed to figure a way to use them.

Because I tie a lot of hair bullet-head flies, something along these lines seemed logical. I tied the feather fibers over the eye of the hook and stroked them back after I tied the fly's body. With a little practice, I could make these flies indistinguishable from those with wrapped hackles. I can tie flies down in the 20s if I want—and the longer the fibers on the feather, the easier to they are use. I learned it was actually quicker to tie flies in this fashion than it was to wrap hackles conventionally. The two important things for this style of tying are making a thorax to spread the hackle fibers away from the body and teaching yourself to manipulate the fibers with your thumbnail to make them surround the hook. I sometimes add a trailing shuck or a wing for more specific imitations. Olive, tan, rust, and peacock cover the color spectrum of aquatic insects.

Cement the hook shank and start your thread on the hook. Strip the fibers off one side of a guinea feather. Try to keep the tips even.

Tie in this clump of fibers just behind the eye of the hook. Let it spin around the hook. The fibers are tied with the natural tips facing forward.

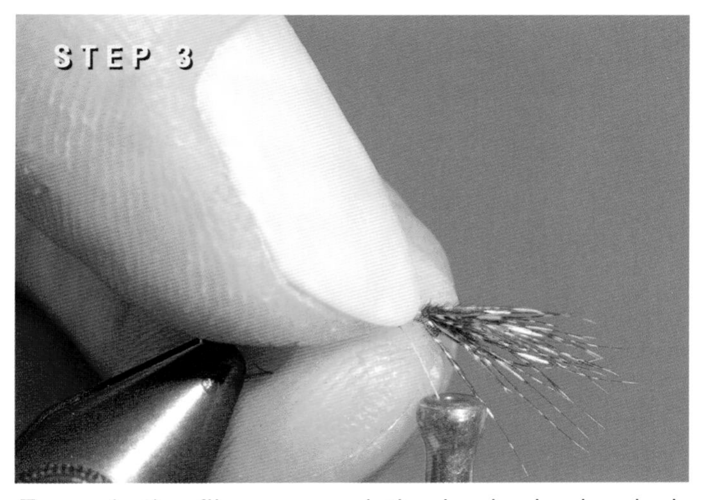

To push the fibers around the hook shank, pinch down on the fibers and hook shank with your thumbnail.

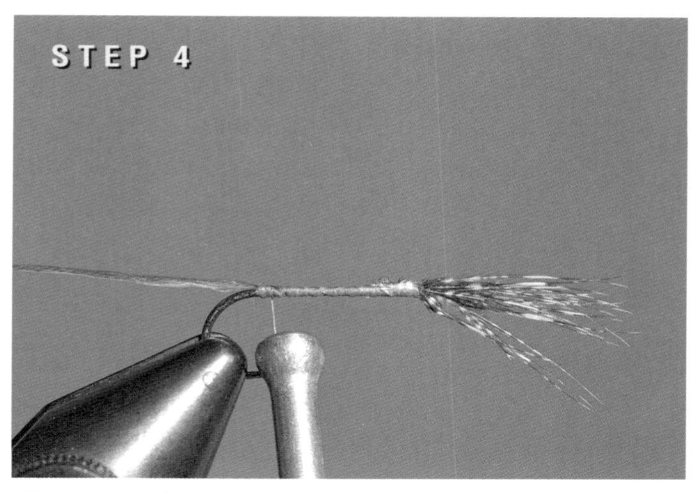

Wrap your thread back to the bend of the hook and tie in a strand of brown thread.

Dub a sparse body to just behind the eye of the hook.

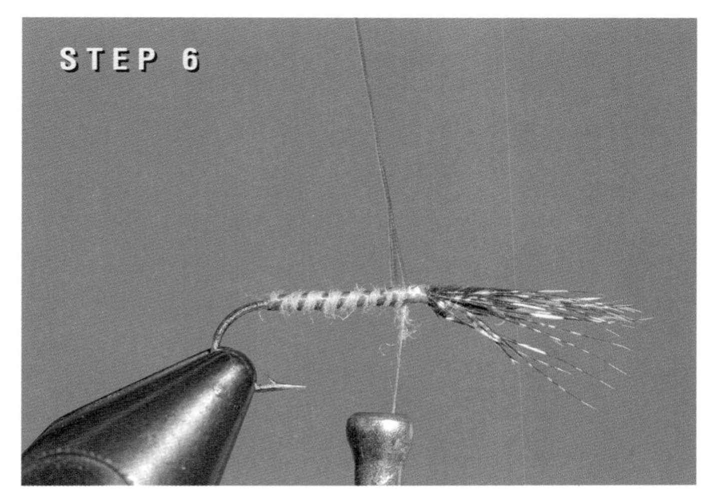

Rib the body with thread and tie off the rib.

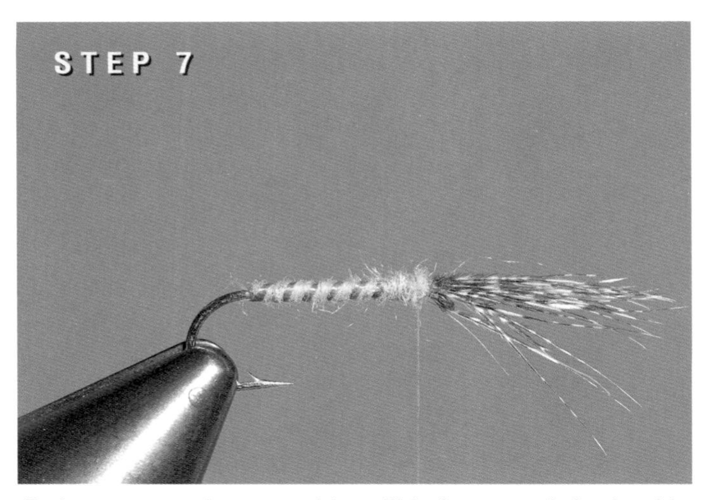

Dub a sparse thorax—this will help spread the hackle fibers in the next step.

Stroke the hackle fibers back to make them surround the body.

Now pull back the hackle and wrap the thread over the butts. Before you completely secure the fibers, you can adjust them by pushing so they flow evenly around the hook.

Finish securing the fibers, whip-finish, and cement.

The finished fly.

DIVING CADDIS OR DIVING BAETIS SPINNER

HOOK:	Dai-Riki 320, sizes 14 to 18.
THREAD:	Olive 8/0.
HACKLE:	Guinea fowl.
RIB:	Brown 6/0 thread.
BODY:	Fine olive dubbing.
WING:	Sparse pearl flash dubbing.

MIDGE & DARK CADDIS EMERGER

HOOK:	Dai-Riki 320, sizes 14 to 20.
THREAD:	Black 8/0.
HACKLE:	Guinea fowl.
SHUCK:	Olive Antron.
RIB:	Pearl Krystal Flash.
BODY:	Scintilla No. 46 Peacockle dubbing.

TERRESTRIALS

DURING SUMMER MONTHS, TERRESTRIAL INSECTS are a significant source of food for western trout. Many of these land-borne bugs are large. They provide a number of calories with very little effort involved in capturing them. Terrestrials are the ultimate cripple: They don't get in the water intentionally. Once wet, they are helpless. Trout aren't ignorant of this and go out of their way to gobble them up.

Streamside conditions on many western rivers are perfect for breeding robust colonies of terrestrial insects. Overall, the West is arid, so consequentially the lives and feeding of many creatures are tied to river bottoms with lush vegetation. From early spring to fall, a variety of land insects are found in streamside vegetation; during the warmest months, they may be the most numerous critters available to the trout.

Foam-Wing Hopper

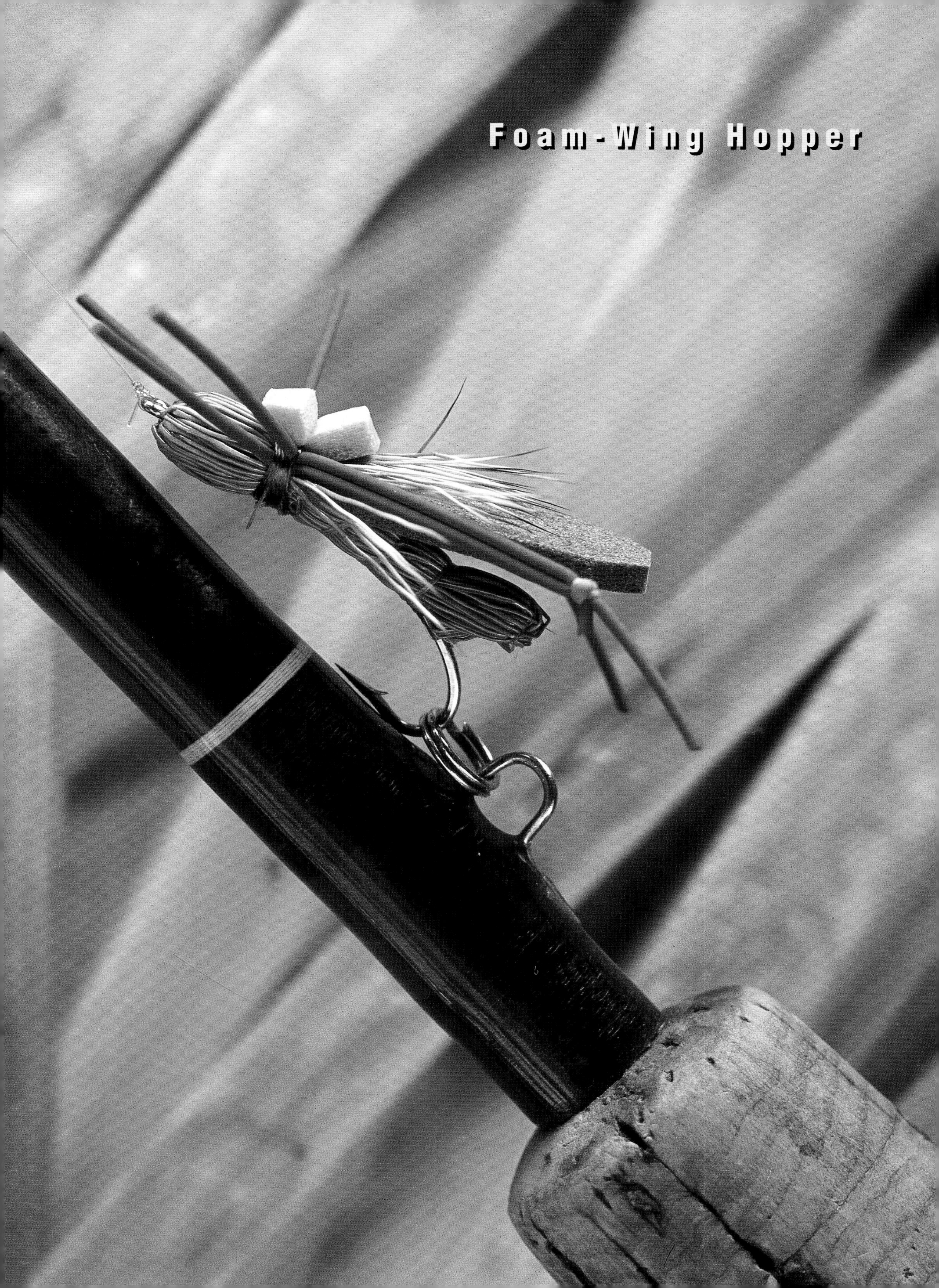

Ants, beetles, and grasshoppers are the most common land insects fed on by trout, but fish are opportunists and feed on others as well. Local infestations can cause fish to key on resident bugs. Sometimes this is cyclical. A particular insect may be abundant one year, then virtually disappear the next.

A little wind or a foraging bovine flushes terrestrials to the water. Agriculture also plays a roll in terrestrial-fishing activity. Haying and other farming practices can cause forced migrations of insects toward the water.

Windy, warm conditions are the ultimate for terrestrial fishing, usually coinciding with times of lean aquatic hatches. In my experience, the middle of the day is the best time. Some of my best terrestrial fishing has been from 11 a.m. to 4 p.m., when many anglers vacate the water and are taking a snooze. The thermally induced winds of July and August are quite strong, often littering the water with terrestrials. One nice thing about these windy conditions and larger flies is that you can fish heavier leaders, which allows you not only to hook fish but also to land them. On clear spring creeks and tailwaters, this gives you an edge

Windy, warm conditions are the ultimate for terrestrial fishing, usually coinciding with times of lean aquatic hatches. In my experience, the middle of the day is the best time.

Some of the best terrestrial fishing occurs on meadow streams. This requires anglers to take advantage of the warm, windy days and make accurate casts next to the bank. Wyoming's Flat Creek is one of my favorites. The smooth water has numerous deeply undercut banks, and the spooky cutthroats will wait in ambush for insects to fall into the water. Their rises are subtle, and the fish typically retreat under the bank after taking a fly.

To fool fish consistently, you need to be able cast next to bank or even under it and then get a good drift—and do this while you are kneeling or crouched. You'll hang up a few flies, but the rewards are worth it. My best afternoon was with a beetle. I landed a dozen fish. Seven of these fish were longer than 16 inches; one was a 24-inch brute. This is on a stream where a couple of good fish a day is considered a success. I've never come close to these results while fishing aquatic imitations.

On the Yellowstone River near Livingston, Montana, you can encounter some terrific hopper fishing, but you need to understand the character of this water to fish it effectively. The Yellowstone's bottom is composed primarily of bowling-ball-sized rocks. Overall, the river has a low gradient along its banks. Depth is the primary cover for the trout. Combine this with the fact that Livingston is the third-windiest city in the country, and you have a situation where you need to fish hoppers away from the bank. Bring your 6-weight. Five or 10—even 20 feet—from the bank is the water to fish hoppers. The hoppers get blown midstream and the fish are there looking for them.

This was different from the tight-to-the-bank hopper fishing I learned in Jackson. Most "foreigners" float where they should be fishing. Luckily, I had experienced anglers as good as John Bailey to show me the ropes. Structure is still important, and irregularities in the bottom and current seams hold the most and best fish. Troughs in tailouts, slight depression off the banks, and rock shelves are prime lies. I joke that if you want to catch good rainbows on the Yellowstone, just look for what you would call whitefish water on most rivers.

Some think fish lack sophistication with hoppers, but this isn't always true. They can be selective about size, color, and profile. It is important to remember that hoppers grow in size through the season. Size 14 may be appropriate in early July—but by October some naturals can be as large as size 4. Many commercial hopper patterns are bright yellow, while most western hoppers are not. Cream, tan, gray, gold, and olive are common natural colors; I like to tie my hoppers in these shades. I think this also helps because so many people fish the yellow hopper that fish can be spooked by it after a time.

While high-floating flies can work well early in the season or over unsophisticated fish, low-floating patterns seem to fish the best. My Foam-Wing Hopper will float for a long time but sits very low in the water—attributes that look good to us and to the fish. I generally use rubber legs on my hoppers. This gives them a nice profile along with some motion. In choppy water, the current vibrates the legs enticingly. You can gently twitch them with your rod as well. Simple streamside observation will give an idea of appropriate sizes and colors for your imitations.

The effectiveness of ants and beetles is remarkable. Small beetles and ants are perfect flies for selective spring-creek fish, but I also fish size 10 to 14 rubber-

FOAM-WING HOPPER

HOOK:	Dai Riki 270, sizes 10 to 4.
THREAD:	Brown Wapsi 140-denier or Danville 3/0.
HEAD/COLLAR:	Dark elk.
BODY:	Long, dark elk or elk rump hair.
RIB:	Gray heavy thread.
WING:	Brown 2 mm craft foam.
LEGS:	Brown, knotted, medium round rubber legs.
INDICATOR:	Chartreuse foam.
ADHESIVE:	Double-stick tape.

My Foam-Wing Hopper will float for a long time but sits very low in the water—attributes that look good to us and to the fish.

leg foam beetles and ants. These flies can pull tough trout from a distance—even after they have refused imitative flies during a hatch. Some may think a size 10 beetle is too big, but a look through the grass may turn up some surpisingly big naturals. The big black silhouette can work wonders. The trout have seen it enough times during their life that they almost instinctively rise to it. I sometimes wonder why I fish any other flies on a spring creek.

Foam-Wing Hopper

Adaptation and modification can be the best innovations. The Foam-Wing Hopper came about as a way to make a longer-floating version of Mike Lawson's Henry's Fork Hopper. It is interesting to note that Mike's pattern was based on Bennett's Pontoon Hopper fished years ago on the Letort Spring Run in Pennsylavnia. Evolution never ends.

The Henry's Fork Hopper is a great pattern for difficult fish. It sits low in the water like a natural. Its only drawback is that because of its low-floating nature, when you catch a fish you typically need to tie on a fresh, unsaturated fly. While this is no big deal when spring-creek fishing, drift-boat fishing doesn't allow this luxury. That could cause you to miss the rest of a good hopper bank.

Years ago I played around with foam-bodied hoppers. My experience was that they floated well and caught the easy fish. However, when the fish grew

tough, my foam hoppers received lots of refusals.

During the 1991 One-Fly competition, Denny Anderson asked me to tie him a bombproof and permanently floating Henry's Fork Hopper. I modified the original pattern by replacing the hen-feather wing with a foam wing. I was pleased with the results, and the fish liked it, too.

The Foam-Wing Hopper has accounted for many memorable days of fishing. One was particularly good.

During 1995, I was living in Austin, Texas while my wife went to grad school at the University of Texas. I came up to Jackson to work at Jack Dennis Sports for a few weeks, guide the One-Fly, and the hit the Fly Tackle Dealer Show on the way home. I planned a week of fishing before I had to work.

I wanted to spend one day on the South Fork. As luck would have it, my friend Clif Williams, who guided on the stream, had a day off. Alvin DeDeaux from the Austin Angler was in the area, so I invited him along. We floated the canyon—a 25-mile trip—in one day. Clif said the hopper fishing had been good, but with this distance of float we wouldn't have time to get out and wade. I rowed first, and when my turn came up I knotted on a Foam-Wing Hopper. The hopper fishing started at 8:30 in the morning and lasted until evening. We had banner fishing all day long on the fly. We caught fish off the banks, fish in side channels, and fish on seams. It was a glory day—we simply could do no wrong. We landed and hooked a bunch of 14- to 18-inch cutts.

When some PMDs and caddisflies started coming off, I added a tan Everything Emerger in front of the hopper. The emerger got them up in the riffles and tailouts, and the hopper produced in the other water. At end the day, we caught some nice browns on Double Bunnies. It was a wonderful day with good fish, good scenery, and good friends.

The hopper fishing started at 8:30 in the morning and lasted until evening. We had banner fishing all day long on the fly. We caught fish off the banks, fish in side channels, and fish on seams. It was a glory day—we simply could do no wrong.

I originally tied this fly with polyethylene packing foam laminated to a synthetic wing sheet. I've since switched to 2-mm craft foam. I also added legs and an indicator. The legs have evolved from baling twine, Ultra Hair, and single rubber legs to knotted rubber. When fishing, I dress the collar and head of the fly with floatant and leave the body undressed. This suspends the body below the wing like a half-drowned hopper. The revelation about this fly is that increasing its flotation didn't hurt its flat-water performance.

I tie my Foam-Wing Hopper in a number of colors to match different hoppers and also to show the fish something different on pressured water. The foam wing should match the body color of the hoppers on your water—or at least compliment the appearance of the real bugs.

I try to match the leg color to the body color. Sometimes a slight exaggeration works. For example, a good hopper combination is light elk with tan or cream legs; this looks like some common western hoppers. Natural dark elk with dull chartreuse legs isn't an exact grasshopper match, but it is in the color range of some meadow hoppers, and the half-bright color scheme may attract attention.

My favorite hopper colors are—body color first, leg next—light elk and tan, dark elk and brown, gray and orange or chartreuse, gold and brown, and black and black. These are my standards. For the foam indicator, I use a bright color, but I try to use a shade that roughly matches the hopper color.

Put a drop of head cement on the hook shank and wrap a base of thread on the hook. Clean and stack a clump of dark elk hair about a half the gap of the hook in diameter. Tie in this clump just behind the eye of the hook. The tips should extend over the eye by about one shank length. Leave this here; the clump of hair will eventually form the head and collar.

Wrap your thread back on the hook shank to above the hook point. Take a clump of elk and cut off the tips to even it. The longer the hair, the easier it is to work with. Tie in this clump by the tips.

Hold the elk hair in your left hand and wrap around it with your thread—but not around the hook—to form an extended body. The body should extend one third of the shank length past the barb.

Wrap your thread forward to within one third of the shank length behind the eye.

Split the loose elk into two clumps with your fingers. One clump should be on the near side of the hook; the other should be on the far side of the hook. Pull the far clump forward and lightly secure it.

Pull the near clump of elk forward and secure it. Trim the butts off both clumps.

Take an 8-inch-long piece of the heavy gray thread and tie it in an overhand knot around the hook bend. Pull it tight and slide it up against the body hair.

Wrap the thread forward in a spiral over the body to form segments in the body. Tie this off.

Cut a wing-shaped piece of foam. When tied in, it should extend from just behind the eye of the hook back to where it is even with the end of the body. It should be one hook-gap wide.

Take a 1/4-inch strip of double-sided tape and wrap it around the base of the wing to help secure the foam without cutting it or flaring it. Tie this on with your thread. You won't need a lot of thread pressure because of the tape.

Pull back the first bundle of elk hair you tied in to form a bullet head and tie it off. Cut off the collar on the bottom to expose the body. Pinch the head with your fingertips from the top and bottom and from the sides. This will slightly elongate and smooth the head. The head will be one third the length of the hook shank.

Knot two connected rubber legs to form legs. Separate the rubber strands on the rear section of the leg and trim one of them off. The back section of the leg will angle down. The doubled legs make a flat surface, which is easier to align than the round surface of a single leg.

Secure a leg to each side of the hook. Adjust and even the legs before you completely secure them. The joint on the rear leg should be even with the hook bend, and the front legs should extend a half a shank length past the tie-in point.

Divide the front legs and wrap your thread between to separate them.

Tie on the indicator above the legs. Whip-finish and cement both the thread and the head.

The finished fly.

Mega Beetle

BEETLES ARE AMONG THE MOST IMPORTANT terrestrial insects for the angler to imitate. Trout see beetles often enough that they associate the shape with food, and I think trout know land-dwelling beetles are helpless once they are on the water. Because of their flat profiles and their tendency to spend time on the ground, beetles frequently go unnoticed by anglers. However, it isn't hard for the fish to see them and they rarely pass them up. Beetles are more common along streams than most anglers think, and their foraging activities sometimes bring them to the water's edge. In addition, there are plenty of other insects that match this shape. Whether the fish take my fly for a beetle, aquatic beetle, box elder bug, or small cricket is immaterial to me, as long they eat it!

Fish don't have as much problem eating a size 10 beetle as the angler has fishing it. The big beetles can attract fish from a distance.

Beetles are one of my go-to flies for tough fish. Trout eat them after repeated refusals of other patterns. They are particularly effective on meadow streams and spring creeks. Many real beetles are small, size 16 or 18, but you would be surprised at the size of others. I've seen plenty of beetles that were a solid size 10 or 12 and a few as large as size 8.

Fish don't have as much problem eating a size 10 beetle as the angler has fishing it. The big beetles can attract fish from a distance. Visibility is another advantage of a larger beetle imitation. This is important when you are stalking spooky fish on your knees or when fishing out of a boat. In areas where many anglers fish hopper imitations, the fish can become picky about hoppers or may even be spooked by them. A beetle is a good alternative.

Beetle seem as if they were designed to be imitated with foam patterns. This material makes it easy to simulate the wide body of the natural. Foam makes flies quick to tie. It floats well and is fairly durable. I'm a rubber-leg junkie: Rubber creates a nice profile, and the subtle motion imparted into it by the river's current looks like a landlocked insect making its last struggles in the water.

Visibility is an issue with a flush-floating black fly, and indicators are a good solution to the problem.

MEGA BEETLE

HOOK:	Dai-Riki 320 standard dry fly, sizes 8 to14.
THREAD:	Black 6/0.
UNDERBODY:	Peacock Angel Hair or Lite Brite.
BODY:	Black 2 mm foam.
LEGS:	Black small round rubber.
INDICATOR:	Orange or lime 2 mm foam.
HACKLE:	Grizzly dyed olive, brown, or green.

The foam indicator on the Mega Beetle also doubles as a platform for a parachute hackle. One problem many foam flies have is a tendency to land on their sides or backs. The parachute hackle adds enough air resistance to make the fly land right side up most of the time. The tie-off technique used on the fly reinforces the hackle at every half turn without requiring extra time to do it.

In areas where many anglers fish hopper imitations, the fish can become picky about hoppers or even spooked by them. A beetle is a good alternative.

Another problem with foam that I've addressed on this fly is body twisting. Foam flies without underbodies easily rotate on the hook shank. The Mylar dubbing provides a good base for the foam and as a bonus gives off some of iridescent sheen found in naturals. Black is my standard color for this fly, but brown, green, and olive are other good colors. The underbody around the body, indicator, and tie-in point will get covered with thread. This is normal and nothing to worry about.

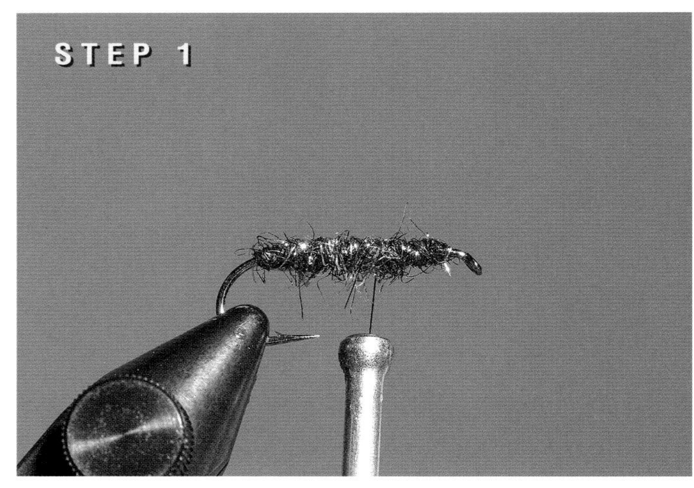

Super-glue the hook shank and make a base of thread. Dub the entire shank with Mylar dubbing for the underbody. When you finish the underbody, your thread should be onethird the shank length in back of the eye.

Cut a foam oval for the body. It should be one and half shank-lengths long and one hook-gap wide. Shape it to look like an egg.

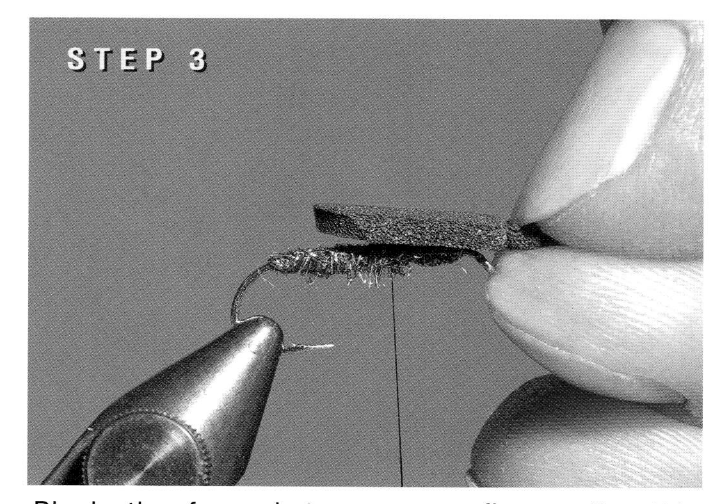

Pinch the foam between your fingernails—this compresses the foam so it is easier tie in.

Tie the foam on top of the underbody one third the length of the hook shank behind the eye. With the fine thread, use multiple wraps under moderate tension to secure it.

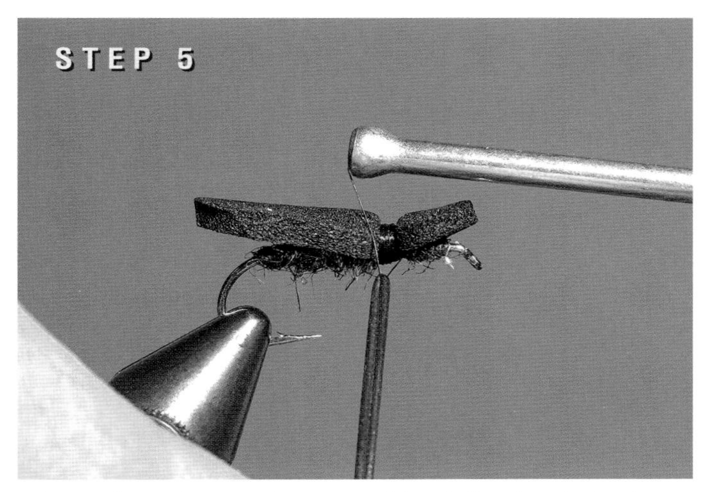

Tie a rubber leg on the near side of the fly at the foam tie in-point. The legs should radiate out one shank-length from the tie-in point.

Tie a rubber leg on the far side of the fly as you did in the previous step.

Tie the foam indicator on top of the body. Lash it down in the center so it forms a wedge.

Tie in a hackle on the side of the indicator above the rubber legs.

Wrap the hackle around the base of the indicator.

To tie off the hackle, wrap your thread through the hackle and the indicator, thus reinforcing the hackle at every half-turn.

Wrap your thread forward behind the eye of the hook and whip-finish. Cement the whip finish and thread around the tie-in point.

The finished fly.

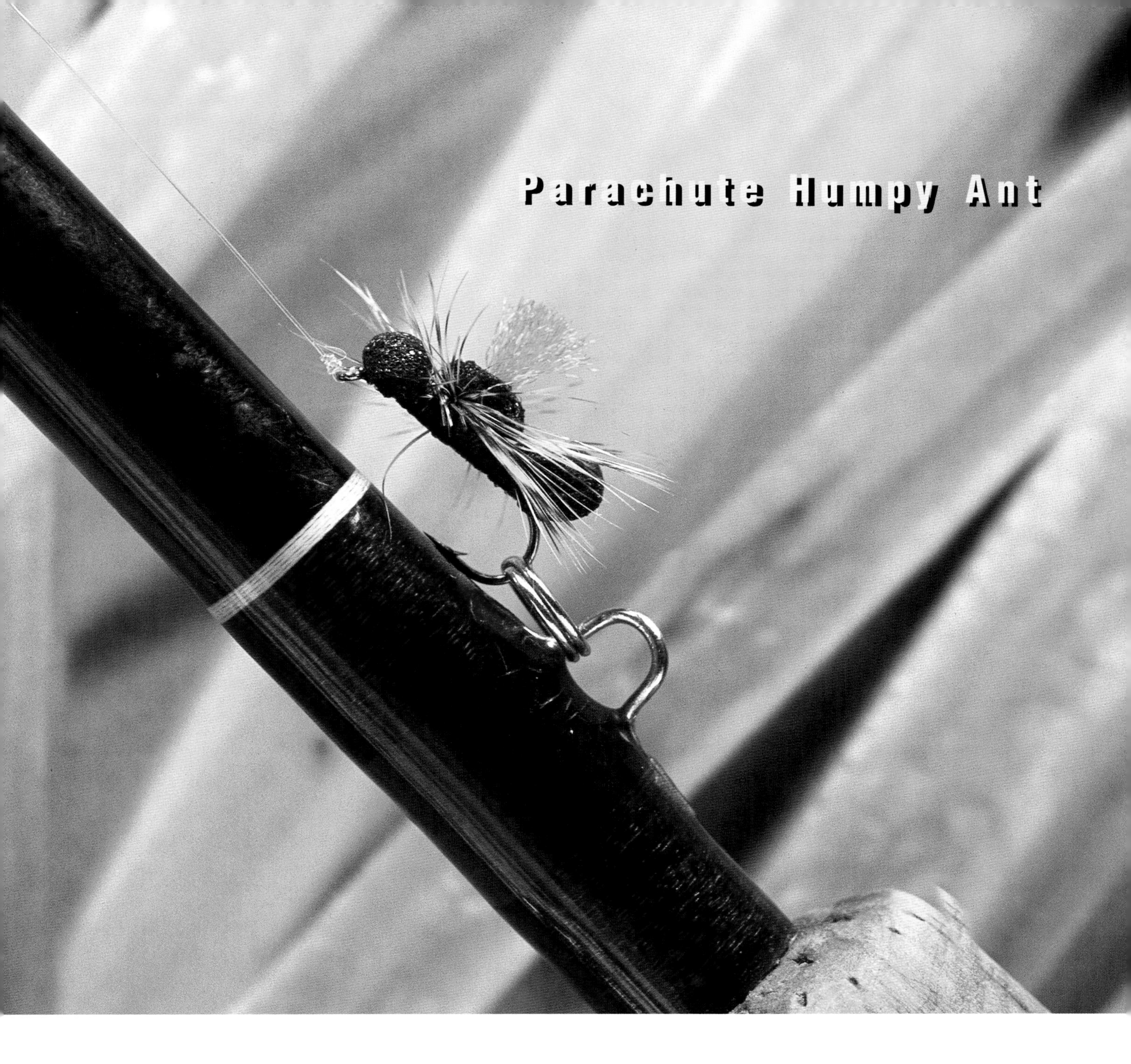

Parachute Humpy Ant

WYOMING'S SNAKE RIVER IS A DIVERSE FISHERY. You can be fishing streamers in the main river and minutes later be fishing through a hatch in a side channel. Much of this variety is caused by the ever-changing river. The Snake has an unstable floodplain. Every year after runoff, new channels are created while others are lost. In addition, as water levels drop through the summer, some channels become fishable and others are lost. The Snake is a schoolroom that never closes.

There are many theories about trout's affinity for ants, but the only vital piece of information for the angler to remember is that when ants are on streambanks, fish eat them.

Side channels are nourishing habitat for our native cutthroats. The reduced water velocity gives them more holding water and, proportionately, there is more overhead cover than there would be in the main stem of the river. Overhead cover in the form of bank vegetation or snags is important to fish that live in a world filled with avian predators such as eagles, ospreys, and herons. Some side channels are large and you need a boat to cover them, but many are like small streams or spring creeks.

Another thing bank structure does for the trout is bring them food. Terrestrials live in the grass and bushes, and it is only a matter of time before one falls in the water. The Snake is certainly not sterile, but it doesn't produce as many insects as rich tailwater fisheries do, and terrestrials are among the principal sources of nourishment in the summer.

Every year, you find some new, big "pet" fish in side channels. The first time you catch them, they are pretty easy to fool, but on return visits they can get tough. Hoppers or big stoneflies will fool them occasionally. During hatches they can be caught on mayfly or caddisfly imitations. But the one fly they seem to like to eat anytime is an ant. I like to use a small foam ant. There are many theories about trout's affinity for ants, but the only vital piece of information for the angler to remember is that when ants are on streambanks, fish eat them. And you should fish ant patterns.

I have Gary "The Wedge" Wilmott to thank for turning me on to ants for tough fish. The Wedge was one the best guides in Jackson. He consistently

PARACHUTE HUMPY ANT

HOOK: Dai-Riki 320 standard dry fly, sizes 10 to 18. (On small flies the Dai-Riki 125 emerger hook works well.)

THREAD: Black 6/0 or 8/0. Flat, shiny threads such as Wapsi 70 or Danville Flymaster make the prettiest underbodies.

BODY: Black foam.

INDICATOR: Fluorescent Antron.

HACKLE: Grizzly dyed brown.

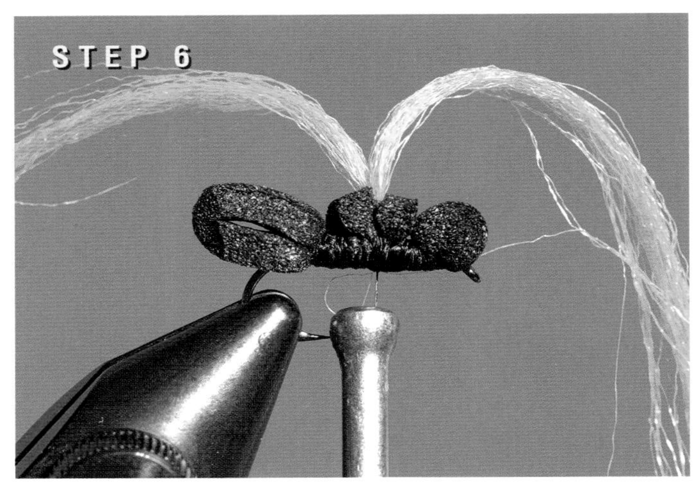

With a finger, push down in the center of the foam strips. Then take a strand of colored Antron, put your thread around it in the middle, and pull it down in between the foam strips. Secure the Antron with thread.

Trim the indicator to as long as the gap of the hook.

Tie in a hackle along the side of the foam strips. The easiest way to do this is to set the butt of the hackle against the foam and hold in place with the thumb of your left hand. Next, push down on the rear foam strip and indicator with your left index finger to open them up. Run your thread over the hackle stem and through the center of the foam strips.

Wrap the hackle around the base of the foam strips and tie it off. You will need to slightly "weave" the hackle around the head and abdomen foam.

Pull your thread up under the body and around the hook eye, and then whip-finish.

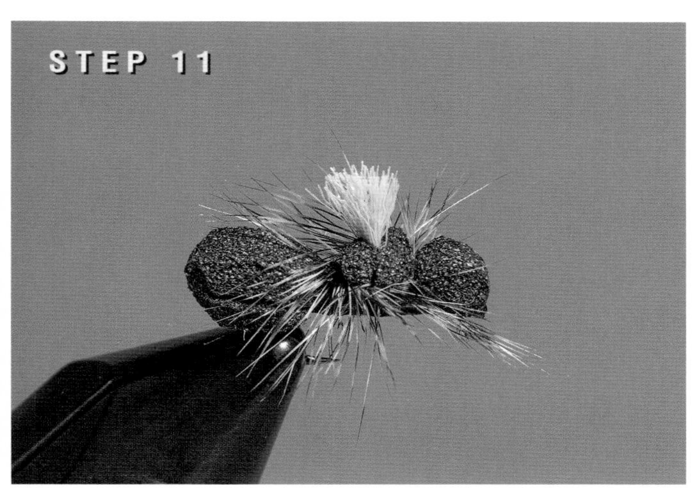

The finished fly.

CHAPTER 8

ATTRACTORS AND CROSS-IMITATORS

ATTRACTOR PATTERNS FORM A LARGE GROUP OF FLIES fished in the Rockies. At one time not too many decades ago, they were the only flies fished on some waters. With the dramatic increase in imitative patterns during the 1970s and 1980s, and better knowledge of aquatic entomology among average anglers, we sometimes forget about these effective flies of yesteryear. The fact is—they worked. And there are situations today when attractors are just what the trout are asking for.

My contemporary patterns in this category are labeled attractors, but I like to call them cross-imitators. While they don't look exactly like anything, they look like a lot of things. Good attractors have attributes that resemble different life forms. They trigger a feeding instinct in predatory fish. For lack of a better term, they are lifelike. When fished properly, they create the illusion of something edible that's getting away.

The Convertible

Attractors are durable workhorses during non-hatch periods and as searching patterns. There are plenty of times when nothing is hatching or there is only random insect activity. This is the time to fish these flies. The fish may not be keyed in to a specific food source, but it is a rare time when a trout can't be enticed with a meaty mouthful.

An effective attractor pattern has a slightly ragged look. Its elements should trigger an immediate response to chase and kill. When no water bugs are emerging or mating, a more subtle match-the-hatch, insect-imitating pattern may not stir an instinctive predatory response in the fish. It's out of place. The timing is wrong. So it's ignored.

I think trout are curious creatures. They are a lot like a little kid who has to touch everything and explore. Since they don't have hands, they use their mouths. In my youthful days of keeping trout, I was surprised at the different objects that I found in trout stomachs: bottle caps, gum wrappers, berries, cigarette butts. I attribute this to curiosity. Curiosity may have killed the cat, but it sometimes catches the trout! These flies are some of my first choices when fishing new, unknown waters.

Cross-imitators are good during multiple-hatch situations. In late April on the Yellowstone River, there is a time of transition between hatches when you'll find a potpourri of midges, blue-winged olives, and caddisflies on the water. In current- and wind-riffled water, I turn to my Midge Convertible. It's superb as a searching pattern while I'm trying to find working fish and for fishing out of the boat between pods of fish. Sometimes I might need to switch to a more exact imitation as I work a pod, but many times I don't. With its down-wing, up-wing, and peacock-colored body, it is close enough to all the insects that most fish will eat it. It floats forever, is easy to see, and doubles as a strike indicator.

If you have seined a stream for insects or flipped over river rocks, you know there are many similarities in the nymphal forms of various aquatic insects. Before turning over one rock in trout stream I've never fished before, I can be sure it's home to insects that are tan, gray, olive, or a mixture of those colors. I know they'll be segmented, heavier in the thorax than the abdomen, and most likely will have some legs. There is also a good possibility that most of them will be between size 18 and size 12. With that knowledge, a fly of those colors and that universal body shape should work in almost any trout stream. It usually does. Generic, buggy nymphs are among any angler's most productive flies. My Ultra Zug nymphs fills this niche in my fly box; friends and I have fooled fish with them on five continents.

With these flies, I can go anywhere in the world and know that I should be able to catch trout.

The Convertible

The Convertible was born from the need for a versatile One-Fly pattern. The Jackson Hole One-Fly competition happens in early September on the Snake River in Wyoming and Idaho. The bulk of it is on the Wyoming side, where the beautiful, native fine-spotted cutthroats make up almost 100 percent of the wild trout population.

This prestigious event allows an angler to fish one fly for each day of the contest. If you choose the wrong fly, your fly comes apart, or you lose it—you're out.

An effective attractor pattern features a slightly ragged look. Its elements should trigger an immediate response to chase and kill.

I've tied many of the flies for the One-Fly. I needed a fly for my clients that would cover multiple conditions, multiple hatches, and relieve the hysteria of having to choose a single fly. It's wild how people who make high-dollar corporate decisions every day can be brought to their knees by the momentary dilemma of which fly to tie on to fool a lowly trout. Fly fishing is a huge priority.

One-Fly conditions on the Snake sometimes make it difficult to choose a fly. Mornings are very cool in

THE CONVERTIBLE

HOOK: Dai Riki 320 standard dry fly, sizes 8 to 14.

THREAD: Rust-brown UNI 8/0.

TAIL: Elk mane, one shank length.

BODY: Fine tan dubbing over the rear two thirds of the shank.

RIB: The tying thread, doubled.

LEGS: Brown medium rubber legs, two and a half shank lengths.

WINGS: White calf tail. The Trude wing should be one and a half shank lengths and the Wulff wings one shank length.

HACKLE: Grizzly and brown, one and a half hook gaps.

I've tied many of the flies for the One-Fly. I needed a fly for my clients that would cover multiple conditions, multiple hatches, and prevent the hysteria of having to choose a single fly.

September; ice in the bottom of my boat is common. And cutthroats don't wake early unless nature gives them a reason. This makes dry-fly fishing slow before midday. Most hatches occur in the afternoon, so streamers are a good choice for the predacious Snake River cutthroats. Also, *Claassenia* stoneflies—large, nocturnally emerging insects—can motivate the fish, making rubber-leg nymphs a good option. As the day warms, insects and the fish become more active. *Hecuba* mayflies, similar in size and appearance to a March brown, caddisflies, and hoppers come into play. Pale morning duns and blue-winged olives appear in some sections of river. This conglomeration is a tough bill for a single fly to fill, and for One-

Fly '91, I had the daunting task of creating a new "super fly."

It made sense to base the fly on existing proven patterns. The ability to trim it down was a given. My answer was to put together a Woolly Bugger/Tarantula/Trude/Wulff.

I wanted the fly to become a Wulff when it was trimmed down, since Wulffs look enough like mayflies to work and are excellent Snake River attractors. To give it bulk, I decided to tie in a large Trude-style wing and then use the butts to form the Wulff wing. A marabou overtail was added for the streamer look, and of course it had to have rubber legs.

I spent the summer testing The Convertible against proven flies. Good news: It kept even with or close to the standards. Surprisingly, the marabou tail fished well dry. I guess the trout might have taken it for an injured insect. I trimmed the fly and fished it in different forms with very good results. The fly was ready for the real test.

During the 1991 and '92 contests, various anglers fished the fly with success and were pleased with its versatility. In '93, Bob Slamal of Riverside, California, used the Convertible to compile the highest point score ever for one day. He fished the fly intact with the marabou tail for the entire day—the fish were doing backflips to get it. I needed a name for it and Convertible seemed logical. One year when fishing was tough, Brian O'Keefe fished it intact, then trimmed his fly to a Trude, a spinner, and finally a nymph. Not many flies offer that versatility.

Since its creation, the Convertible has become one of my favorite attractors. It has evolved into a set of patterns. By pure accident, I came up with a fly that imitates fluttering insects. Stoneflies, caddisflies, damselflies, and dragonflies all have two sets of wings that are spread when flying. Also, the profile of lots of wing and legs with a sparse body is similar to that of a cranefly. During heavy caddisfly hatches, I think it's eaten as a caddis cluster.

I hear stories from other anglers about the Convertible: brook trout and rainbows in Vermont, cutthroats and bull trout on the Middle Fork of the Salmon, Kentucky smallmouths. Those are just a few. The fly has become a standard in Livingston guides' fly boxes. Bob Slamal calls me every year for a Convertible order to use when guiding around Pinedale, Wyoming.

The Convertible is its own clearly visible, permanently floating strike indicator. It can be fished and tied with or without the rubber legs; different kinds

It made sense to base the fly on existing proven patterns. The ability to trim it down was a given. My answer was to put together a Woolly Bugger/Tarantula/Trude/Wulff.

In '93, Bob Slamal of Riverside, California, used The Convertible to compile the highest point score ever for one day. He fished the fly intact with the marabou tail for the entire day—the fish were doing backflips to get it.

of rubber can be used. For smaller sizes, synthetic wings are an option. Fish it in its entirety or, if needed, trim it to a Wulff or Trude. Without legs, a Convertible doesn't take any longer to tie than a traditional Trude or Wulff. The advantage is that with this single fly you now have multiple flies in your box. Some of my favorite variations are royal, peacock, blue damsel, salmonfly, yellow Sally, and olive.

The Convertible is a fly that puts you in the driver's seat.

Cement the hook shank and wrap a thread base on it. Even the elk mane and tie it in at the bend of the hook for a tail one shank-length long.

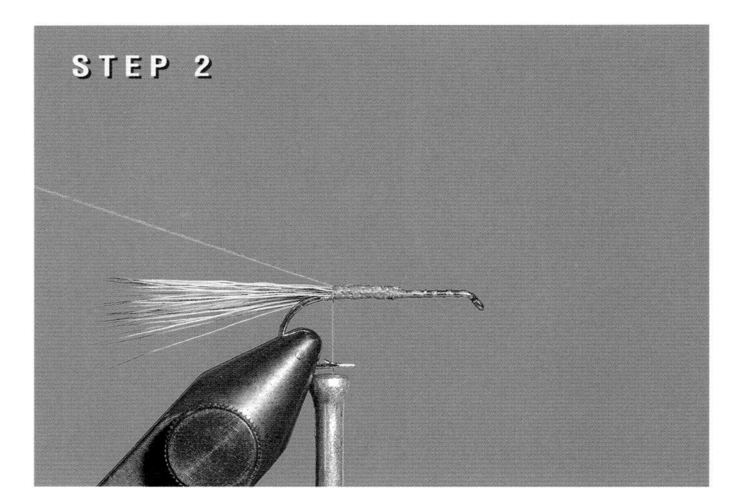

Make a dubbing loop with your thread for the rib.

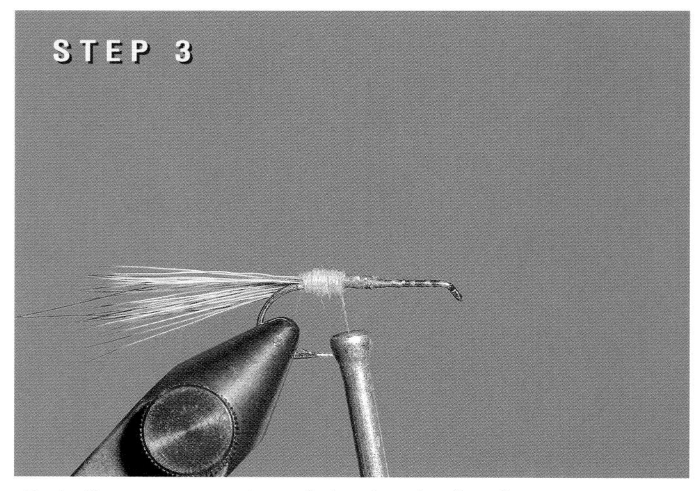

Dub the rear quarter of the hook shank.

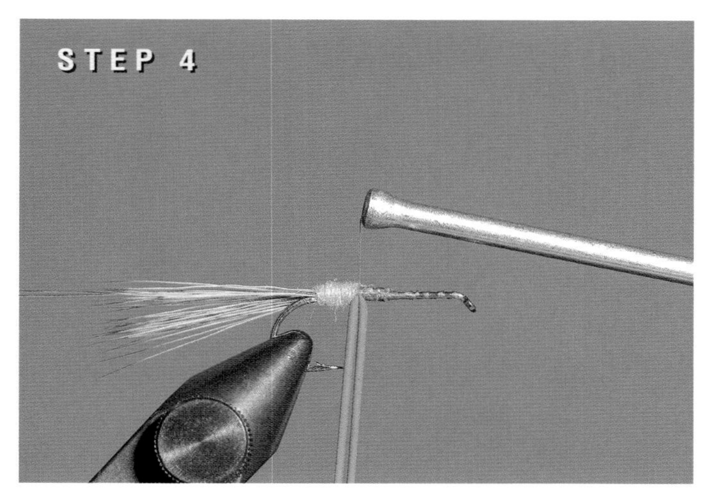

Tie in a rubber leg on the near side of the hook shank. Secure it in the middle of its length so that it flares into an V.

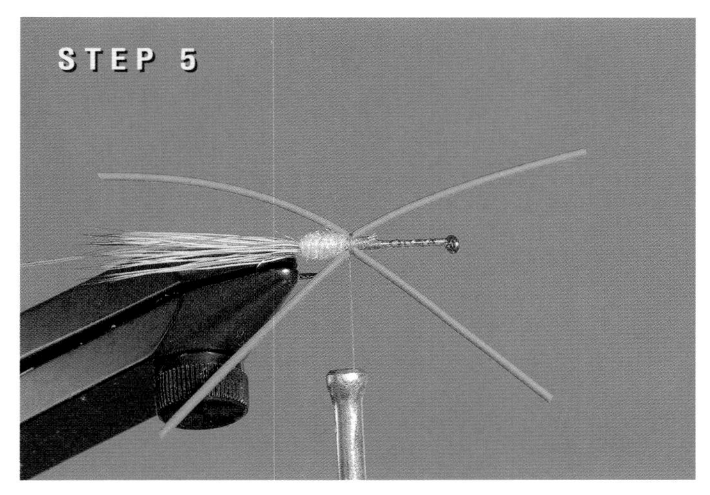

Tie in a rubber leg on the far side of the hook shank. Trim the legs; they should be about two shank-lengths long from the tie-in point.

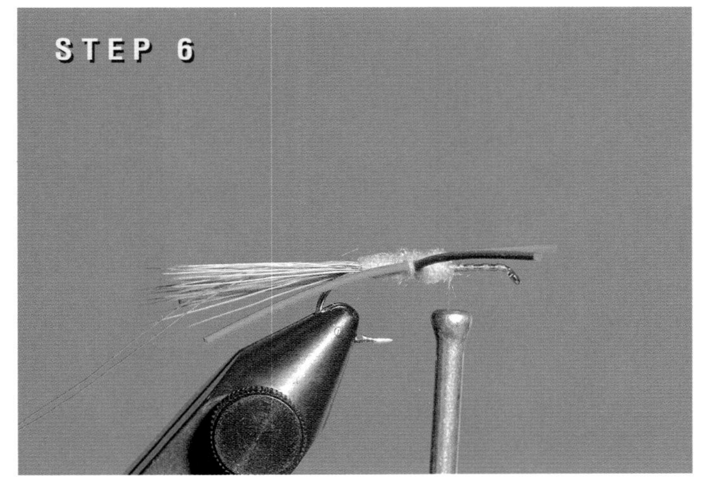

Dub through the legs and then make one or two wraps in front of them; you should now be halfway up the hook shank.

Twist the doubled thread and rib the body with it. Be careful not to trap the rubber legs.

Clean and even a bunch of calf tail. Just in front of the body, tie in a Trude wing that extends even with the end of the tail.

Use the butts of the Trude wing to form the Wulff wings. Wrap your thread in front of the butts to lift them up.

Snip out the center third of the Wulff wing to reduce its profile and to make the two Wulff wings. Post the wings with thread.

Trim the wings to a shank length. I often trim the ends of the Wulff wings to make them slightly uneven and make them look more natural. Taperizer scissors will also work.

Tie in a grizzly and a brown hackle and make five to six wraps through the Wulff wings. Tie off the hackle, whip-finish, and cement.

The finished fly.

ROYAL CONVERTIBLE

HOOK:	Dai-Riki 320 standard dry fly, sizes 8 to 14.
THREAD:	Red Wapsi Ultra 70.
TAIL:	Moose body hair.
BODY:	Alternating Scintilla Peacockle dubbing and tying thread.
LEGS:	Medium black rubber.
WINGS:	White calf tail.
HACKLE:	Brown.

MIDGE CONVERTIBLE

HOOK:	Dai-Riki 320 standard dry fly, sizes 14 to 18
THREAD:	Black 10/0.
TAIL:	Moose body hair, approximately one shank length.
BODY:	Scintilla Peacockle dubbing.
WINGS:	White calf tail.
HACKLE:	Grizzly.

Ultra Zug

SHAGGY, BUGGY NYMPHS AND WET FLIES are deadly patterns. Most of these flies are considered attractor nymphs, but I label them cross-imitators. They aren't an exact imitation of anything, but they are close enough in appearance to many food items. The secret is that the loose fibers give the fly a lifelike profile and a little movement. The dubbing fibers may imitate legs and in some cases hold air bubbles like many emerging nymphs.

The standard technique for tying these flies uses a dubbing loop. This method has advantages and disadvantages. It does make a buggy fly, but it is time consuming and forces many tiers to rely on extra tools.

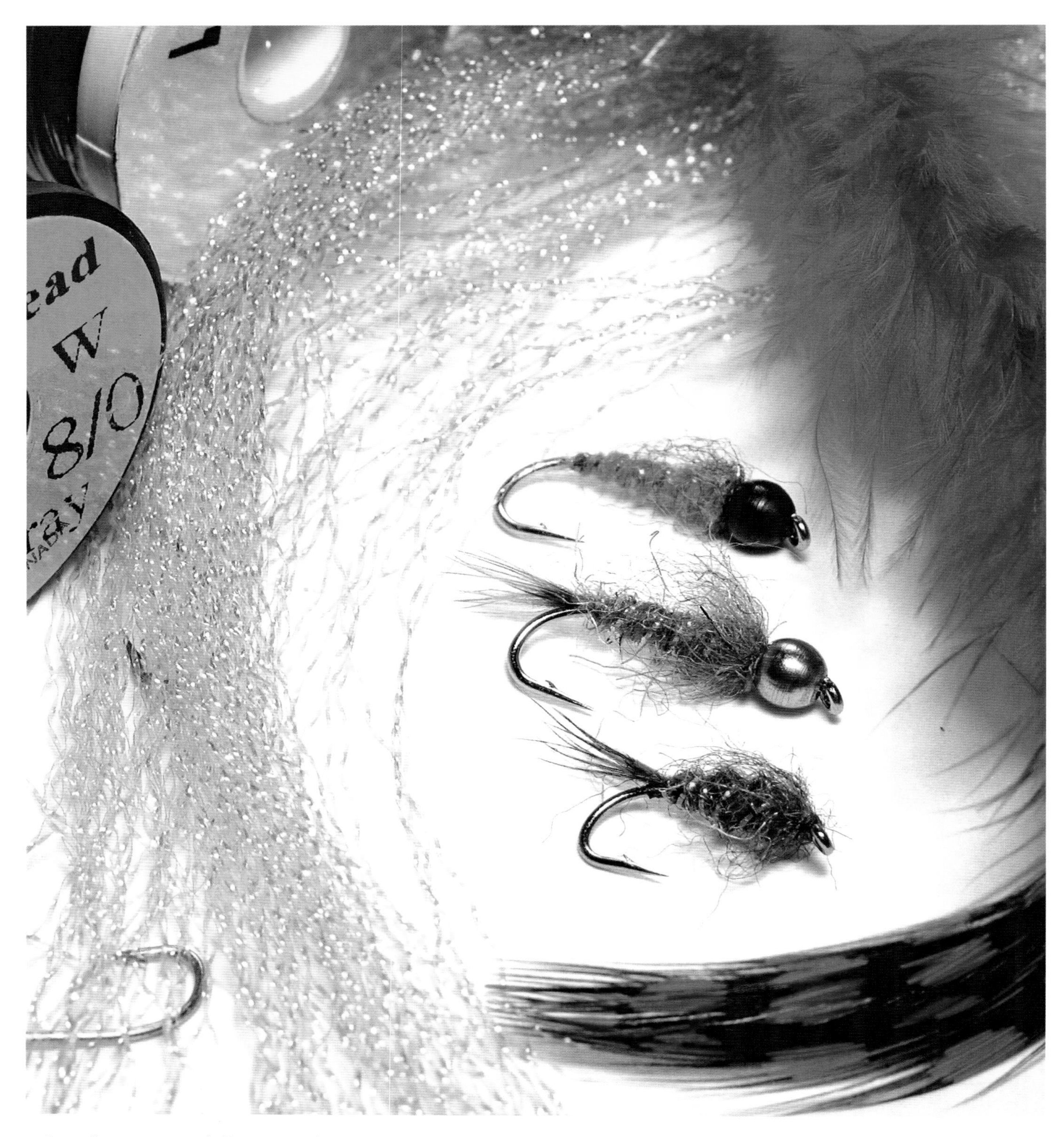

I prefer to use a different technique for these flies: "clump dubbing." This involves fluffing up a clump of dubbing and then lashing the clump to the hook. The technique is similar to spinning deer hair, but it is much easier.

I came upon this method a number of years ago while finishing a commercial fly order. In those days, I worked for Jack Dennis and tied most of the Kiwi Muddlers for his shop. Flaring hair was second nature. It was late one evening after I finished the day's fly order when I remembered I needed some nymphs for myself and a friend to fish the next day. I started tying some Hare's Ear nymphs. To save time, I intentionally left off the wing cases. As I tied, I figured there had to be a quicker way to make a buggy thorax without dubbing it and teasing it out or using a dubbing loop.

Almost on autopilot, I grabbed a clump of dubbing

ULTRA ZUG

HOOK: Dai-Riki 075 heavy-wire wet fly, sizes 10 to 20.

THREAD: Black 8/0.

WEIGHT: A few wraps of lead wire in the thorax area.

TAIL (OPTIONAL): A few short fibers of dyed-green guinea fowl.

BODY: Sparse amount of Scintilla No. 46 Peacockle dubbing.

RIB: A strand of pearl Krystal Flash.

COLLAR: A tuft of body dubbing spun like hair behind the eye of the hook; the ends of the fibers can be trimmed or broken to the desired length.

Almost on autopilot, I grabbed a clump of dubbing and spun it deer-hair style on the hook. The spun fibers gave me the desired appearance.

and spun it deer-hair style on the hook. The spun fibers gave me the desired appearance. To complete the fly, I folded the fibers back with my left hand, held them together and clipped them to length. The finished fly looked good. Over the next dozen, I worked out the technique, and it took very little time to finish the needed flies. I also tied some nymphs with peacock-colored dubbing and called them Ultra Zugs. The next day, John Hanlon and I enjoyed some great winter fishing on the Snake and caught plenty of trout and whitefish on the new patterns. They fished as well as more complicated Hare's Ears and Zug Bugs.

The Ultra Zug is now an old friend of mine, and I have used it as basic nymph template. The color and body proportions can be changed to imitate many insects. Its best attributes are the short amount of time needed at the vise and its universal appeal to fish. Olive, tan (hare's ear), cream, and gray are other good colors for this pattern. Dark heads with lighter bodies are good imitations of various aquatic larvae. It has produced throughout the Rockies, in France, and for transplanted trout in Texas and New Zealand.

Bead-head variations have followed the Ultra Zug's inception. An unweighted fly is a good caddis emerger. I tie the fly with soft, multicolor synthetic sparkle dubbings such as Scintilla and with a pearl Krystal Flash rib. The translucent rib takes on the color of the body and gives a lifelike gleam. I often give an Ultra Zug a short soft-hackle tail.

It works well in moving water, but has really proved itself in Montana and Wyoming lakes. High-mountain lakes can host very heavy evening midge hatches. Surprisingly, during this phenomenon, the fish you might think would be easy can be difficult. Fish seem to key on the rising pupae instead of the adults. Floating flies go unnoticed. A size 14 to 18 Ultra Zug retrieved with very short strips is more effective than any other pattern I have used on these still waters. On Jenny Lake in the spring, I have even caught mackinaw on this fly. Sight-casting to fish in clear water is exciting, and the added rewards of casting to beautiful fish in scenic surroundings are hard to beat.

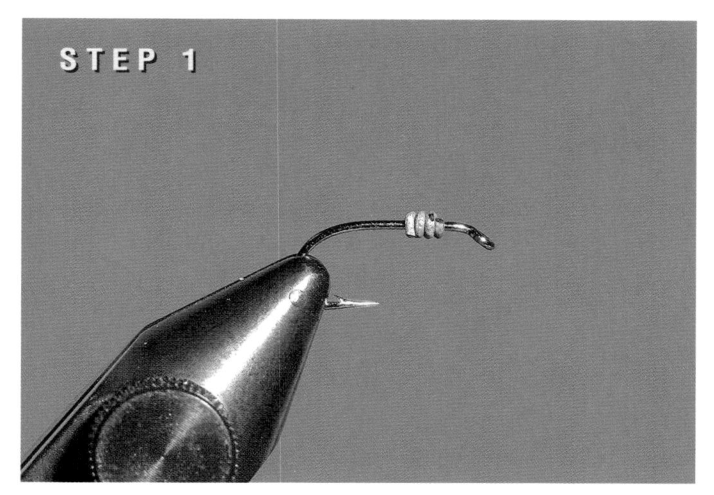

Make two to four wraps of lead wire in the thorax area.

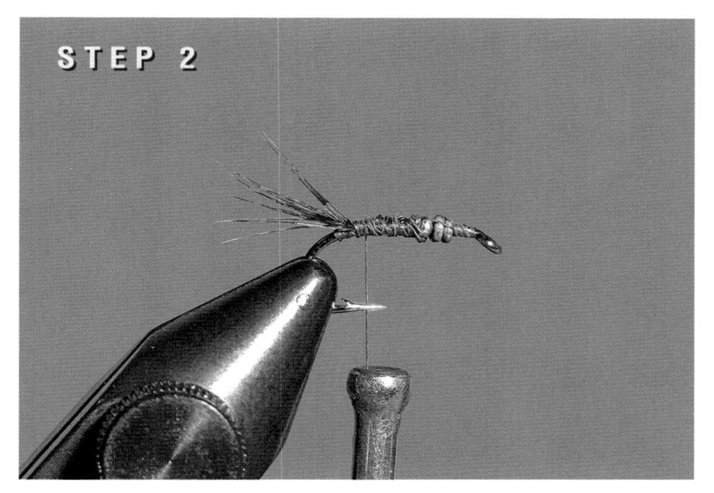

Cement the hook shank and start the thread. Tie in a small clump of guinea fibers about half a hook shank in length.

Tie in a strand of pearl Krystal Flash for the rib.

Dub a sparse body that covers most of the hook shank and the lead wire.

Rib the body with the Krystal Flash and tie it off.

Spread a sparse amount of dubbing between your left thumb and index finger and then hold it against the hook shank just behind the eye of the hook.

Secure the dubbing with your thread and let it spin around the hook shank.

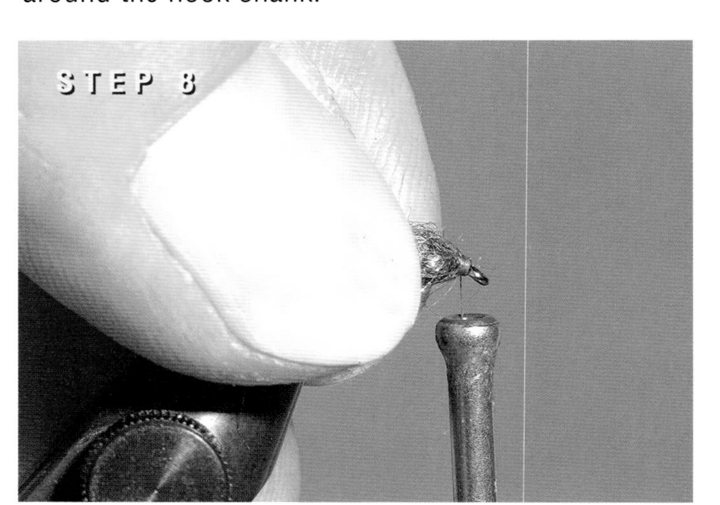

Stroke back the fibers that went over the hook eye, fold them back toward the bend, and secure them.

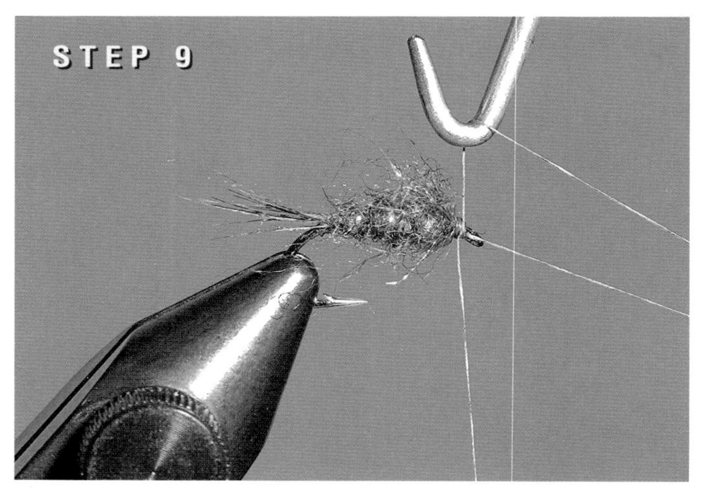

Whip-finish and cement.

Comb out the fibers with your scissor tips and cut them off. They should form a sparse, short collar. Try to make the ends uneven.

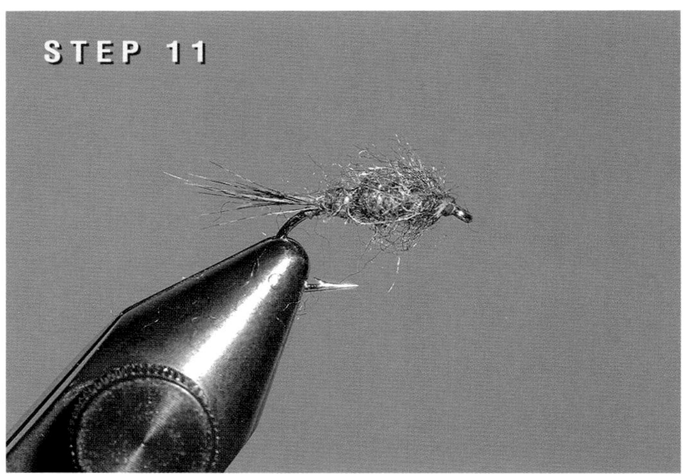

The finished fly.

ULTRA ZUG FREE-LIVING CADDIS

HOOK: Dai-Riki 060 heavy-wire wet fly, sizes 10 to 16.

THREAD: Black 8/0.

WEIGHT: Black metal bead.

BODY: Lime dubbing.

RIB: A strand of pearl Krystal Flash.

COLLAR: A tuft of Peacockle dubbing spun like hair behind the eye of the hook; the ends of the fibers can be trimmed or broken to length.

ULTRA ZUG HARE'S EAR

HOOK: Dai-Riki 060 heavy-wire wet fly, sizes 10 to 16.

THREAD: Brown 8/0.

WEIGHT: Copper bead.

BODY: Synthetic hare's-ear dubbing.

RIB: A strand of pearl Krystal Flash.

COLLAR: A tuft of body dubbing spun like hair behind the eye of the hook; the ends of the fibers can be trimmed or broken to length.

CHAPTER 9

STREAMERS

IT'S NO SECRET THAT BIG FISH EAT LITTLE FISH. For anglers seeking larger trout, fishing streamers is the ticket to success.

Fish attack streamer patterns for two basic reasons: to eat them or out of territoriality. The motivation of food is pretty straightforward and understandable, but the aggression issue is often overlooked.

Trout, especially larger ones, take the best lies in a river. They can be very aggressive when defending their homes. In low-water conditions on Wyoming's Flat Creek, I've watched large trout protect their lies. In one instance, a group of whitefish swam around a particular cutthroat until they got too close. Then the cutthroat bit or body-slammed the whitefish as they drifted a little too close for comfort.

Double Bunny

I have also watched spawning brown trout chase competitors out of their turf. Some of the best streamers for brown trout in the fall have brown and yellow in their color schemes. I believe they work because they are the same color as the hormone-charged browns, and the trout mistake the streamers for parr invading their domain. Like all predators, trout are conditioned to attack an easy meal; a streamer placed near them can cause an instinctive attack-response. Seemingly lethargic fish can in a fraction of second become active predators.

I can remember as a 13-year-old reading *Trout* by Joe Brooks, and being captivated by his descriptions of catching huge fish in the Yellowstone River and in South America. I knew I needed to try it. I spin-fished

Like all predators, trout are conditioned to attack an easy meal; a streamer placed near them can cause an instinctive attack-response. Seemingly lethargic fish can in a fraction of second become active predators.

when I was a kid and knew how effective minnow imitations could be on spinning tackle. Brand-new lures, however, depleted my modest budget—but I could tie flies for almost nothing. I tied up some Brooks Blonde flies and tried them for myself. I rode my bike to fishing adventures whenever I could. I can't say I knocked them dead, but I caught fish.

Later in life when I first went to work for Jack Dennis, I was introduced to streamer fishing out of a boat with some of the newer patterns. I started fishing extensively and frequently with many of the best guides on the Snake, Green, South Fork, Salt, and New Fork Rivers. I also quickly learned to row a boat. (You won't fish with a guide on his day off if you don't become adept at the oars!) The shop was always in need of more of Jack's Kiwi Muddlers, since they weren't a commercially tied pattern at the time. I filled in and made a fair amount of money tying Kiwis in my spare time. I became pretty good at cranking them out. Thus started my long affair with rabbit-fur streamers.

When you cast streamers from a boat on a river with good bank structure and snags, the challenge is to quickly put your fly next to cover and then make it come alive. Everything is moving. You don't get many second chances. Hung-up flies usually can't be rescued; they must be disposable. In some ways it's like high-speed bass fishing. It's fun, though, when a dark shape darts out from under a log and follows your fly as you scream, "*Eat it!*"

I like rabbit flies for this fast-paced fishing. They look alive when stripped or dead-drifted. Sometimes I like to fish two flies at a time and give the fish a choice. Hey, why not help them figure out what they want to eat that day? A common combo for me is a Yuk Bug or Rubber-Leg Bugger and a Double Bunny. I like to believe that the fish think the Bunny is a small fish trying to eat a stonefly nymph, and they either take the stone away from the small fish or try to knock the small fish out of the way.

My best-known fly, the Double Bunny, came about because of saltwater fishing. Saltwater fishing gives you penetrating and frequent looks into streamer fishing and forage-fish predation. Lessons learned in the tropics, combined with my experiences with trout, inspired me to create an effective new pattern and a Rocky Mountain standard. Warmwater fishing also influenced my ideas. Trips for pike, bass, and other warmwater critters have given me opportunities to fish baitfish imitations in a variety of situations. All have expanded my view at the vise.

When I became involved with Dan Bailey's Fly Shop as a fly-pattern consultant, I learned to fish streamers in a different way. Owner John Bailey learned to fish with Dan, his father, and Dan Bailey's frequent partner, Joe Brooks. On the Yellowstone River flowing through Livingston, Montana, deep pools, runs, and troughs are the best bets for large trout. I joke around that the Yellowstone's browns are allergic to wood.

To cover this big water efficiently, Joe Brooks and Dan Bailey used 8- and 9-weight rods with sinking shooting heads and mono running lines. They borrowed their technique from West Coast steelheaders: Wade out as far as you can, make a cast as far as you can, and let it sink. When the fly begins to swing, strip it. For this style of fishing, lighter-weight flies are easier to cast with a shooting head. I like rabbit for much of my streamer fishing, but feather and

DOUBLE BUNNY

HOOK:	Dai-Riki 700, size 2.
THREAD:	White Gudebrod G.
WEIGHT:	.035 lead wire on the front half of the hook shank.
BODY:	White Magnum Rabbit Strip for the belly; chinchilla Magnum Rabbit Strip for the back.
SIDES:	Pearl Krystal Flash and silver Holographic Flashabou.
EYES:	6 mm molded 3D eyes glued on with Goop.
ADHESIVE:	Val-A-Tearmender.

bucktail patterns are easier to cast. They also sink deeper. And the depth of the fly may matter more than the exact pattern.

Chester Marion, the big-fish guru of the Yellowstone, ties the Marion Spruce Fly, which is one of the most productive patterns for this river. The fly is fashioned with natural grizzly, dyed-olive or dyed-brown grizzly, or badger hackles. A feather wing is combined with a heavy collar made of at least two long hackles. When the fly is held against the current, the collar looks just like a sculpin's head and moves enticingly in the water. I tie mine with a bead head for a little weight and a jigging action.

When throwing streamers, it is important use tackle adequate for the job. Small streamers can be fished on a 5-weight and, out of necessity, I've thrown Double Bunnies on a 3-weight, but a 7-weight is a more practical fishing tool. I'm a 7-weight junkie and own a collection of them. They are useful because they are big enough to do the job, but you can still feel a 15-inch trout. Also, it's the first weight on the scale for which a good variety of sinking lines can be found.

Make sure your leaders are strong enough to withstand vicious strikes or pull a fly from minor snags, and stout enough to deliver the fly. Many anglers see the strength of fine modern tippets and figure that they will work for streamers, but you need some mass to turn over large, heavy flies. Fluorocarbon in 2X through 0X is my favorite. With floating lines, stiff-butted 7- to 9-foot leaders are fine, but with sinking lines, a 5-foot level, heavy tippet will keep your fly down with the line.

Streamer fishing is always effective. Learning a variety of techniques and fishing different fly patterns allows a resourceful angler to catch fish when there's not much going on in the way of hatches. It's your best chance of catching the largest fish in the stream.

Double Bunny

The idea for the Double Bunny came to me almost 20 years ago while on a fishing trip to Belize. John Hanlon and I were trying to catch some barracuda that were not being cooperative. The two flies that ended up working the best were a Kiwi Muddler and a FisHair Cuda Fly.

What would happen, I wondered, *if I put together the pulsating action of rabbit fur and the undulating motion of a 'cuda fly?* I didn't have the necessary materials to tie the Double Bunny on that trip, so it had to wait until I was home.

Some months later, while fishing my home waters of Jackson, I watched a large trout chase a smaller fish on the end of my line. The idea of the "super barracuda" fly instantly came back to me. That night the first Double Bunny popped out of my vise.

The first time I fished the new fly, the lake trout and cutthroats in the Snake River below Jackson Lake were chasing it harder than a politician looking for Florida votes. I've used it successfully ever since. It's a great fly for finding and catching large fish. So far it has subdued more than 30 species ranging from cutthroats to tarpon—even a catch-and-release fly-rod-record channel catfish. The 1992, 1993, and 1994 Jackson Hole One-Fly competitions were won on Double Bunny variations.

The "Hasenpfeffer Emerger" (as a friend calls my Double Bunny) isn't a fly for the timid, but the rewards are great. Most of my flies are 3 to 4 inches long. Because today's fast-action rods generally don't throw heavy flies very well, for trout fishing I normally use a medium-action, 7-weight rod with a sinking-tip, Teeny, or full-sinking line. The fly's rabbit hide and fibers move seductively as it drifts or falls. One of my favorite retrieves is to strip it and let it drift like a dying baitfish. I've found that the eyes on it don't necessarily elicit more strikes, but they do help prevent short strikes. Many predators key in on the eye of baitfish to see which way the fish is moving. In fact, a number of fish species have adapted to have false eyes on their bodies as a defense mechanism.

Originally, I tied the Double Bunny on a stinger hook, sometimes with a trailer hook. Brown trout, lake trout, warmwater, and saltwater species all tend to strike the head of a forage fish, so standard-shank hooks worked fine. As often as not, however, cutthroat and rainbow trout sideswipe a minnow—you'll miss them with a shorter hook. For trout, I've switched to long-shank streamer hooks (Dai-Riki 700, sizes 1 through 4), and I tie the fly on the front half of the hook shank. This allows the fly to undulate as it does on a shorter hook, yet hooks fish that hit the body or head. For warm water and salt water, I use a standard stainless hook (Dai-Riki 930) or a heavy-wire bass hook (Dai-Riki 810), and I sometimes tie in a mono weedguard.

I used to incorporate Zonker strips in the pattern, but wide rabbit strips such as Hareline's Magnum Strips make it easier to cover the lead underbody. If you do use Zonker strips, I suggest you cover the lead with Mylar dubbing such as Lite Brite orAngel Hair.

I watched a large trout chase a smaller fish on the end of my line. The idea of the "super barracuda" fly instantly came back to me. That night the first Double Bunny popped out of my vise.

Because I tie so many of these streamers, I glue entire rabbit hides together and strip them out with a disposable box-cutter knife. I prefer Val-A-Tearmender brand latex contact cement to glue the rabbit hides. It can be bought at hardware and canvas-repair shops, and is distributed to fly shops by Hareline and Freestone Flies. Barge Cement and similar glues also work well, but the fumes can get to you.

My Australian friend, Mick Hall, ties some Mini-Bunnies out of squirrel strips. Wapsi now sells squirrel and mink strips that should work on smaller flies. Rob McLean's new Bar-Dyed Zonker Strips give your flies distinct parr markings or a mottled look.

The numerous color combinations you can tie and fish are limited only by the colors of rabbit you can find. Typical of baitfish patterns, the darker color is tied on top of the fly. The following are effective variations for trout.

1. Chinchilla over white—baby whitefish.
2. Olive over gray—baby rainbow trout and

sculpin (One-Fly winner).

3. Natural brown over ginger—baby brown trout.
4. Natural brown over yellow—Platte River Special.
5. Black over fluorescent yellow—for dirty water and low light.
6. Black over white—Integration Bunny.
7. Dark gray over chinchilla –small trout and sculpins.
8. Black over ginger—for low water, bright light.

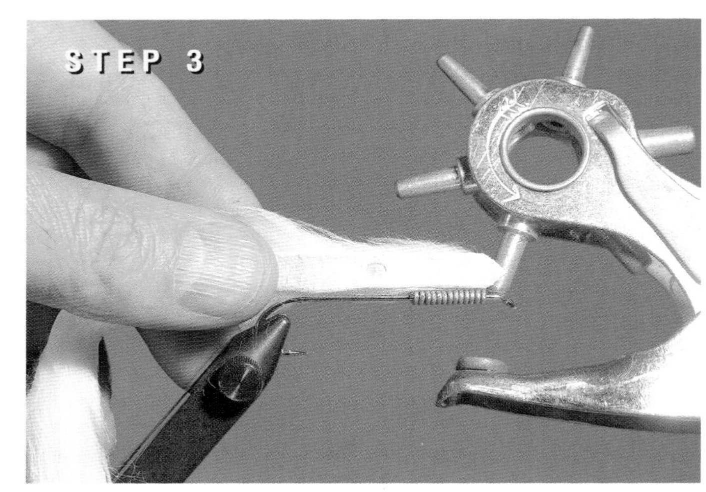

With scissor points,a knife, or a leather punch, pierce a hole in the belly strip one and a half shank lengths from the tip. This will allow you to pre-weight hooks. You can also impale the belly strip with the hook.

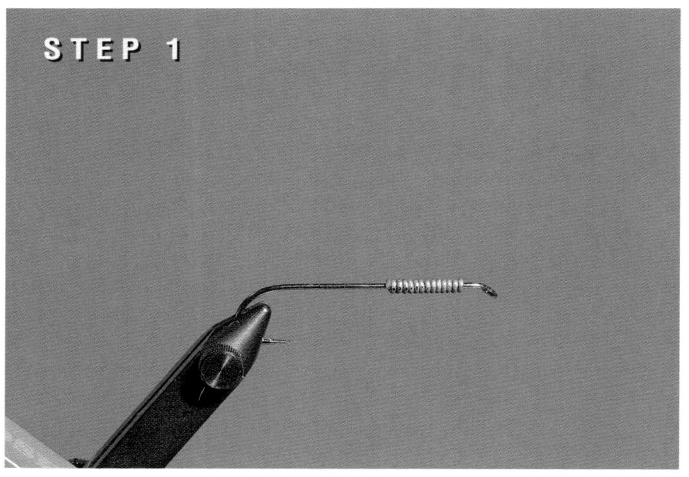

Wrap .035 lead on the front half of the hook.

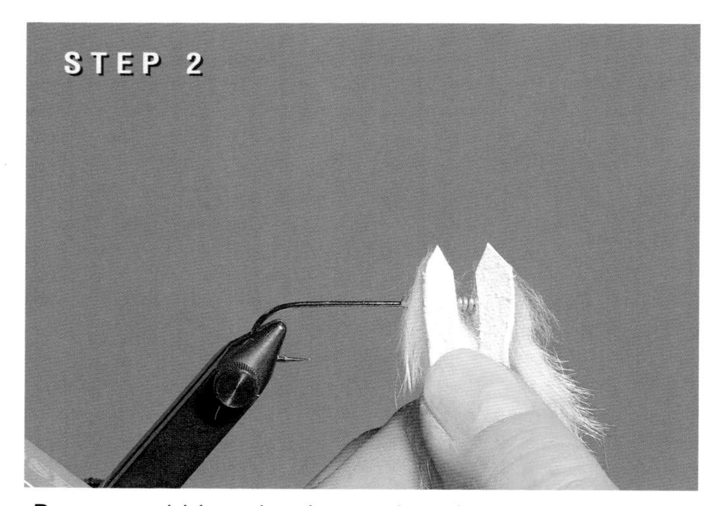

Prepare rabbit strips by cutting the tip of each to a point.

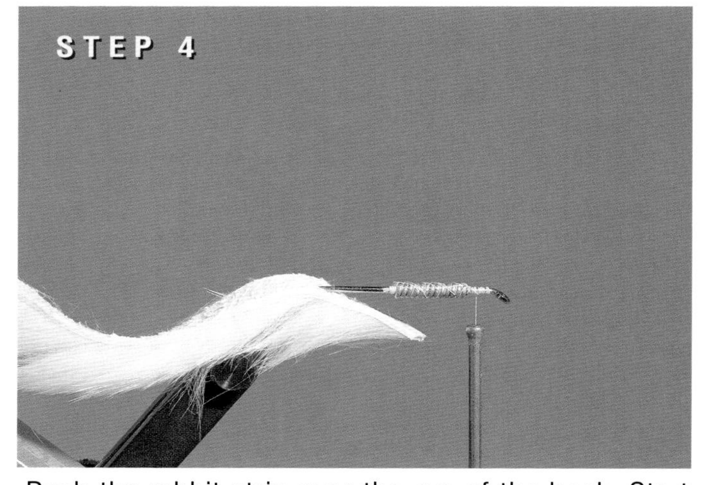

Push the rabbit strip over the eye of the hook. Start your tying thread and secure the lead. Lash some loose rabbit fur to the lead to help the glue bond and to cover the lead. (You can use Mylar dubbings such as Lite Brite as well.)

Tie the bottom rabbit strip by the tip just behind the eye. Hold the fur out of the way with your left hand to prevent trapping it.

Secure the top rabbit strip by the tip. Hold the fur out of the way with your left hand to prevent trapping it.

Holding the back end of the top rabbit strip away from you, use a toothpick to apply a *light amount* of contact cement on the hide only—if you put too much on the toothpick, you risk getting it on the hair.

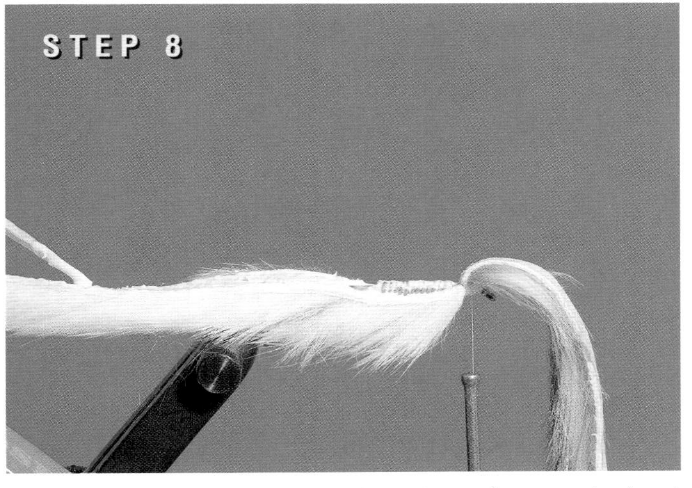

Coat the hide side of the belly strip and cover the lead with contact cement.

Hold the tail ends of the rabbit strips in your left hand and pull them straight back. With your right hand, pinch the strips together and down onto the lead.

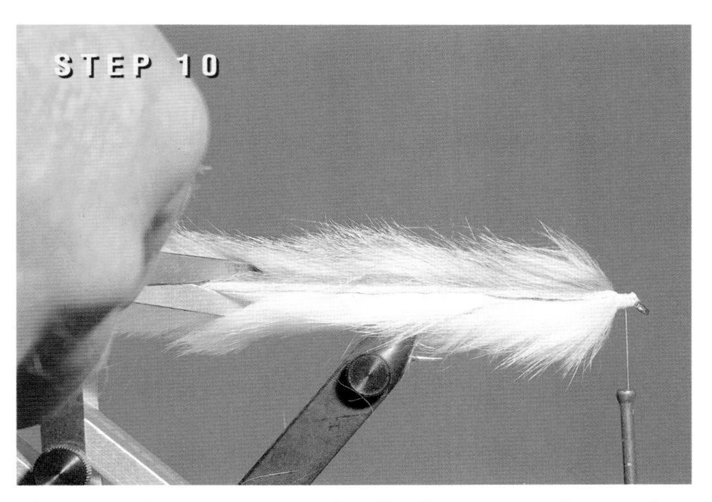

Cut the body to length. Push your scissor tips through the hair to prevent cutting off the fur.

Rotate the fly so that the top faces you. Cautiously taper the tail so that it is lighter and more flexible when wet. Slide your scissors and cut just a little at a time.

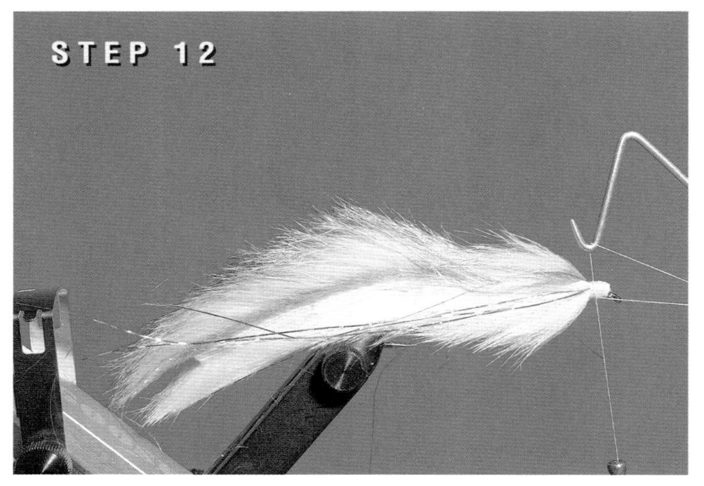

Take a few strands of Krystal Flash and Holographic Flashabou that are double the body length and tie them in at their midpoint just behind the hook eye. Next, pull the forward-facing material to the far side of hook and tie it in place. Cover the ends with thread, whip-finish, and cement.

Attach the eyes. Stroke the rabbit hair back. With a toothpick, coat the area just behind the thread head with Goop.

Place an eye on the glue. Repeat this on the other side. Make sure you use enough glue to hold the eyes.

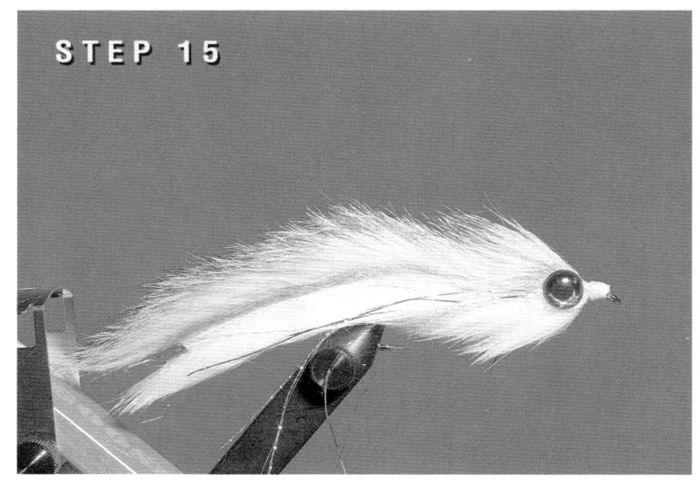

The finished Double Bunny.

There are a number of good choices for Double Bunny eyes and heads. Stick-on eyes can be used in place of the 3D models, but you still need to make a glue base. I epoxy over the head and eyes for more durability, and to add weight to the front of the fly. EZ Sparkle Body or acrylic T-shirt paint can also be used to build up a head and reinforce it. Some commercial versions use dumbbell eyes. Orvis sells a Conehead Double Bunny. When using cone heads, place the cone on first and then tie the fly. Use some lead behind the cone and super-glue it to keep the body from sliding back as you fish the fly.

One of my favorite head-eye combos uses heart-shaped pony beads from a craft store. They have a large hole in the center that fits over the eye of the hook. To use them, finish the Double Bunny up to the whip finish. Take a bead and slide it over the hook eye to make sure it fits on the fly without blocking the eye. Then put a drop of super glue on the hook and slide the bead back on. With the bead affixed, you can now stick on the eyes. Use stick-on eyes or adhesive 3D eyes that are smaller than the side of the bead. These beads come in many colors; clear beads will work with any color scheme.

Clump-Dubbing Leech

MOHAIR LEECHES ARE KILLER STILLWATER AND RIVER FLIES. They may not be exact imitations, but they have enticing motion and a lifelike profile. In my experience, they outfish that universal standard streamer, the Woolly Bugger. I don't know if mohair leeches work because they have a profile that the fish haven't seen or because the yarn fibers move in the water, but I'm always happy to give the fish what they want to eat. I frequently use a leech as a backup for a Double Bunny.

Sometimes a fish will turn and chase a big streamer but won't come back. Many times I've switched to a smaller leech and fooled a trout that had turned down a bigger fly. I also use the Clump-Dubbing Leech as a light-rod streamer. On the Snake, I fish a lot of large dries, but I'm always ready to switch quickly to a streamer. A size 8 Clump-Dubbing Leech fits the bill, and I don't need to switch leaders or rods to fish it.

Sometimes a fish will turn and chase a big streamer but won't come back. Many times I've switched to a smaller leech and fooled a trout that had turned down a bigger fly.

Mohair yarns work well on leech patterns, but they come in a limited range of colors, and the fly is limited to a body diameter the size of the yarn. Coarse dubbing spun in a loop is frequently used for leeches, but I'm not a big fan of the time required to form a dubbing loop to complete what should be an instant fly.

The Clump-Dubbing Leech is a descendent of my Ultra Zug nymph, the pattern on which I first used clump dubbing. This method seemed a logical choice for leeches. It gives me unlimited options for the color and size of the fly. Another benefit to this technique is that different sections can be tied in different colors to create a mottled fly. Sparser versions can be used as traditional leeches, baitfish, or generic damselflies, while heavier dressings make effective sculpins, baitfish, or dragonfly nymphs.

To control the bulk of the body, tie in larger or smaller clumps of dubbing or vary the spacing of the clumps. Bulk can also be controlled by teasing out the fly more aggressively and pulling off more dubbing. These techniques can be varied along the hook shank to create a taper.

The fly should be trimmed after teasing out the dubbing. A trim top and bottom will make a great-swimming leech that planes and undulates in the water column. A trim on the sides gives it a flat baitfish profile. If you desire, add eyes to the baitfish.

This clump-dubbing method is best accomplished with long-fibered materials. I like synthetics such as Scintilla and Wapsi Antron Sparkle Dubbing, and blends such as Wapsi's Crawdub—they work on a wide range of fly sizes. Mohair and mohair blends such as Stalcup's Leech Dubbing, Angler's Choice Mohair Plus, and Arizona Simi Seal are excellent on

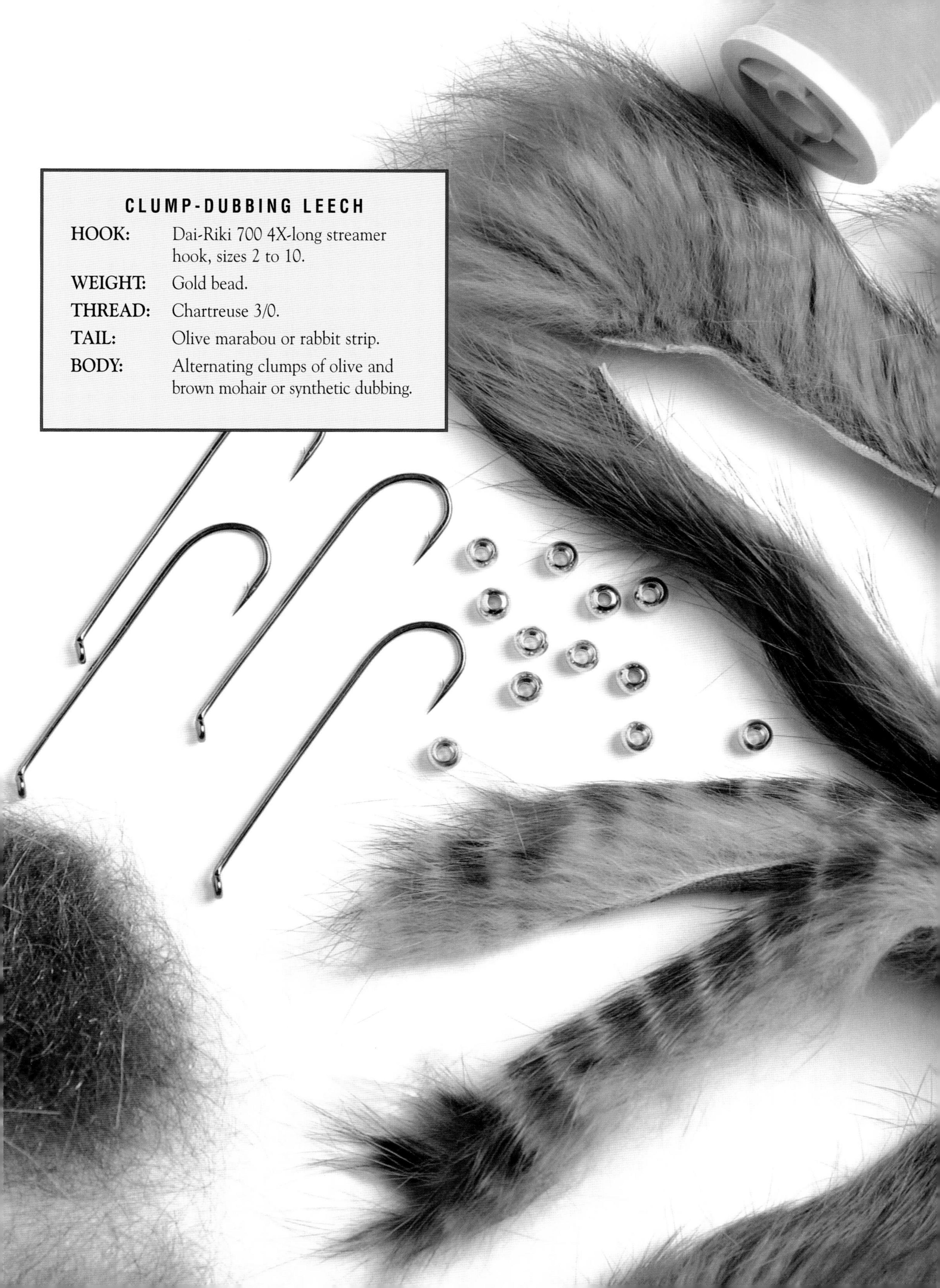

CLUMP-DUBBING LEECH

HOOK: Dai-Riki 700 4X-long streamer hook, sizes 2 to 10.

WEIGHT: Gold bead.

THREAD: Chartreuse 3/0.

TAIL: Olive marabou or rabbit strip.

BODY: Alternating clumps of olive and brown mohair or synthetic dubbing.

leech patterns and other large flies. Mylar materials such as Lite Brite, Ice Dub, Polar Dub, Holo Bright, Fire Star, and Ultra Holographic dubbing can be used for these flies or blended with less reflective materials. Natural dubbings with guard hairs, such as hare's-ear blends, can be used in this fashion on smaller flies. Doug Swisher's Rub-A-Dub dubbing from Montana Fly Company has "guard hairs" of rubber strands and is best applied with this method.

The fibers should be approximately twice as long as the desired length of the collar. Tiers who want to make their own dubbing in a blender should cut the base material fairly long. Acrylic knitting yarns are a good base material.

Bead heads or cone heads are the easiest weighting options for these flies, as a bare hook shank will make it easier to spin the dubbing. However, an underbody of lead wire can be used alone or in conjunction with a bead head.

Standard colors for the Clump-Dubbing Leech are olive, black, peacock, purple, rust, tan, and gray.

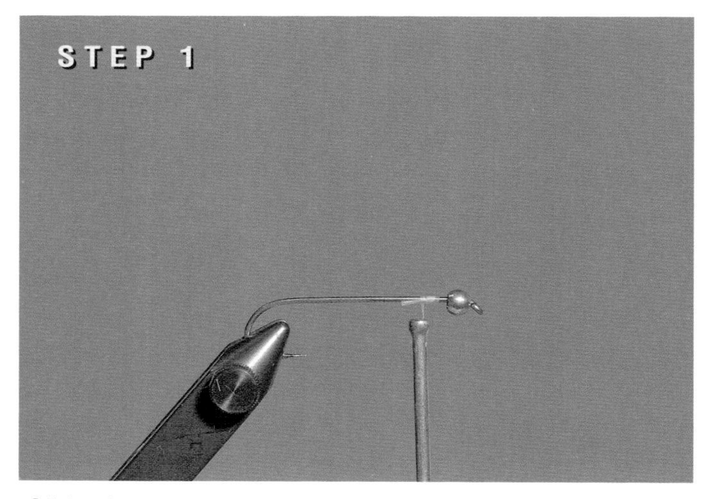

Slide the bead on the hook, cement the hook shank, and start your thread.

Tie in a tail of marabou or rabbit equal to the length of the hook shank.

Pinch a clump of brown dubbing between your thumb and index finger. Rub the dubbing between your finger and thumb to spread it into a rough circle.

Fold the dubbing around the hook shank so that it envelops the hook. Secure it to the hook with your thread and let it spin around the shank.

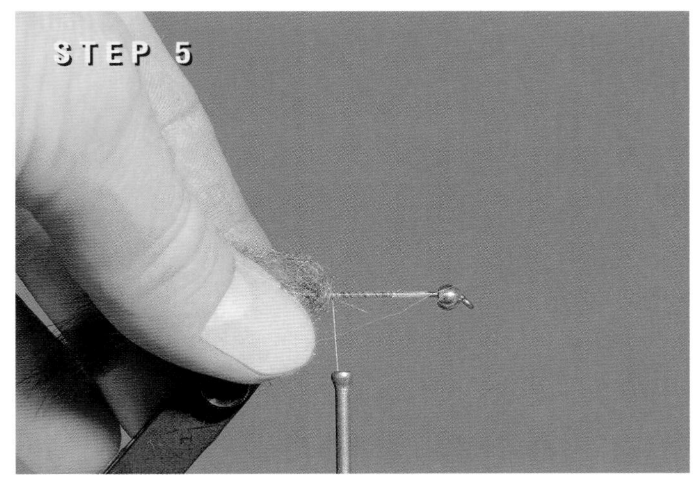

With your left thumb and index finger, stroke back the dubbing that faces forward, and fold the fibers back toward the hook bend. Use your thread to secure the fibers back.

Spin a clump of olive dubbing in the same fashion you did the first clump.

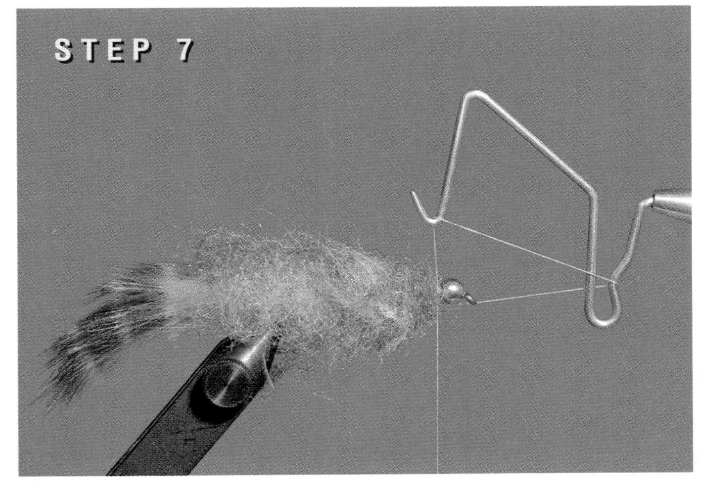

Continue the clump-dubbing sequences until the shank of the hook is completely covered. Whip-finish and cement behind the bead.

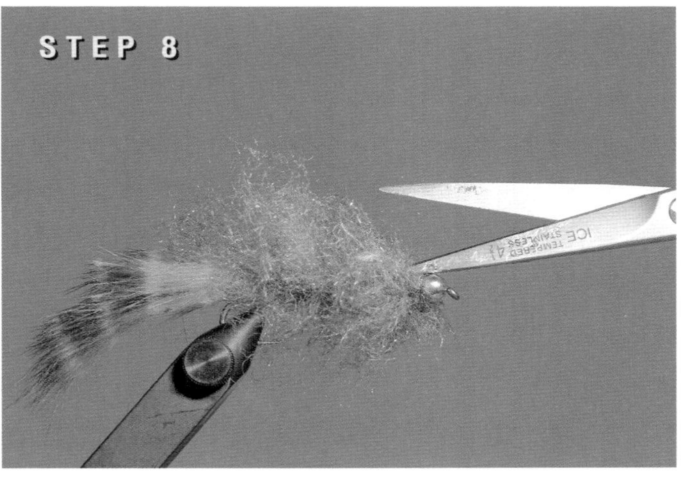

Push a blade of your scissors or a heavy-duty bodkin through the dubbed body to untrap and pull out extra fibers; this loosens up a fair amount of material.

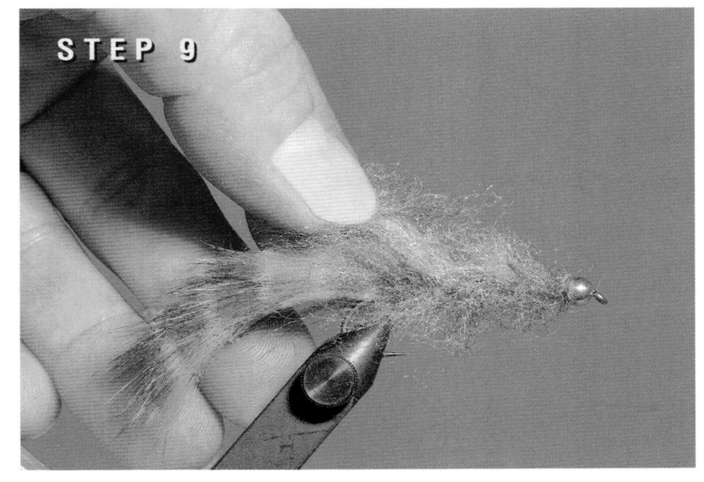

Pull off the loosened fibers with your fingers and save them for the next fly. Be careful not to poke your finger when doing this. When the Leech looks even and it is adjusted to your tastes, the fly is finished.

The finished Clump-Dubbing Leech.

AFTERWORD

As we reach the end of *A New Generation of Trout Flies*, I hope you have enjoyed sharing my ideas and perspectives about fly tying. Others have influenced and inspired me through personal contact and their writings, and I hope this text leads you down this same road of discovery. Human interaction and communication are amazing things.

New materials appear; tying techniques change. Fishing tackle evolves; trout become more sophisticated. This progression presents new challenges, but it also creates the opportunity for ever-new accomplishments.

Angling success can be measured by different scales: the number of fish caught, the size, the difficulty of tricking a particularly smart trout. But to me, the constant is having fun. Yes, the catching is important. So is the experience. The sound of a stream, a crimson-purple sunset, the grin of your son with a God-awful fly in his vise or a fish on his line, the certainty that a new fly you are tying on a minus-10-degree day will fool the trout that eluded you last summer—these are as important as a 30-fish day.

With fly tying and fishing much is constant. Yet much changes. And both lead to enjoyment. In the spirit of the Robert Earl Keene song, "The road goes on forever and the party never ends."

INDEX